INTERPROVINCIAL CO-OPERATION
IN EDUCATION

INTERPROVINCIAL CO-OPERATION IN EDUCATION

THE STORY OF
THE CANADIAN EDUCATION ASSOCIATION

Freeman K. Stewart

W. J. Gage Limited, Toronto

1957

CONTENTS

Part III

The Canadian Education Association Since 1948

Introduction

Canada is the only country, except Switzerland, which has neither a national ministry of education nor a federal office of education; all other countries, whether organized politically as unitary or as federal systems, have some official central educational agency. Even Switzerland, with which Canadians like to compare Canada in this matter, has had, since 1891, what is called the Standing Conference of Heads of Cantonal Departments of Education. Financed by the cantons, this conference has certain recognized responsibilities for the provision of educational information and liaison services.

In view of the unique position in which Canada finds itself in comparison with other countries, it was considered desirable to make a study of the efforts made by educationists since Confederation to find some means by which they could meet together to exchange ideas, learn of each other's progress and failures, and arrange for national reports on educational developments and trends.

Except for the preparation of educational statistics, which, like other statistics, is the responsibility of the federal government, the provincial departments of education have come to look primarily to the Canadian Education Association for at least preliminary discussions of matters which are of concern to more than one of them and on which they would like to exchange views. The CEA may not often be needed for this purpose, but on such occasions it is invaluable. However, if the CEA or some other agency met only on occasions of this nature, it would not be possible to convene a satisfactory *ad hoc* meeting; in order to have a reasonably useful appreciation of each other's problems and points of view, it is necessary that there should be not too infrequent personal contacts and casual exchange of ideas, both of these being basic to the establishment of mutual confidence and respect.

Probably, although officials of the departments of education are not often very conscious of it, the existence of this need constitutes one of the important reasons why the departments support the CEA by financial contributions in proportion to provincial populations. There are, of course, other and more obvious reasons for interprovincial support of the CEA, and these are set forth in the story that follows.

While the CEA is supported by tax funds, it is none the less a voluntary organization from which any participant may withdraw at any time. The following chapters trace the history of the CEA and attempt to explain, by reference to its history and current activities, how educationists happened to form the Association and the provinces ultimately to support it.

After discussion of some topics of special interest and a brief report on methods of educational liaison at public expense in three other federal countries, an examination is made of the various functions of the CEA as a voluntary agency in a federal state.

It is rather remarkable that no study has previously been made of the long history of the Canadian Education Association, for it is generally regarded as one of the most influential in Canadian education. In fact, the CEA has been relatively little known until recently outside a limited circle of school administrators, partly because it has never solicited funds from the general public for its maintenance. The CEA, like the British Commonwealth, is held together by ideas and ideals more than by logic, and this is not always discernible to an outsider nor the story properly told by reference to written records alone. It is therefore hoped that this small volume will provide a useful source of information about the organization.

The account that follows does not pretend to be either a definitive history of the CEA or a presentation of it in an idealized role. The activities of CEA members in promoting federal aid for technical and agricultural education, and subsequently what was called vocational education, are not explored. For one reason, these activities are not a part of the CEA's own development; for another, it is difficult, without making a complete study of these matters in themselves, to distinguish the effect of discussions in the CEA from what would have happened without such discussions. It is perhaps sufficient to say that on occasion federal aid in these areas was a popular topic at CEA meetings, and that the views expressed by educationists at such meetings contributed to federal action in providing financial assistance.

Written sources of information about the CEA have been the Proceedings of the Association since its establishment in 1891, the minutes of meetings of the directors and of the executive, and the official journal of the Association, published quarterly since 1945. A study has also been made of the files of the Association, scanty prior to 1945, but fairly complete and unquestionably voluminous since that date. A bibliography is provided (see page 169), but this, of course, fails to reveal the number of publications which might be expected to mention the CEA but do not. A conscientious effort was made to examine contemporary publications for references to the Association, but the result was depressingly unrewarding.

It has been a privilege to include in this book the opinions of three of the most influential figures in the growth of the CEA on the role of this organization, and we feel that the quality and authority of these statements by Dr. J. G. Althouse, Dr. C. E. Phillips, and Dr. B. O. Filteau add considerably to the value of the book.

PART I

The Development of
the Canadian Education Association
to 1948

Chapter 1

THE DOMINION EDUCATIONAL ASSOCIATION IS ORGANIZED, 1891

When the sixtieth anniversary of the Canadian Education Association was being observed in 1951, someone rather sceptically asked what its accomplishments had been during its first fifty years. First of all it can be said that the CEA, under several names, survived as a national organization—no mean feat in a country where travel and communications were often difficult and always expensive. Education authorities have seldom been in a position where surplus funds would enable them to look on such handicaps with indifference, and, in any event, caution in expenditures has long been a characteristic of educationists, if not necessarily a virtue. Nor should it be forgotten that education in Canada is an activity most sensitive to feelings of provincial autonomy and vested rights, so that a program involving more than one province sometimes partakes of the nature of an international event.

None the less, the organization, difficult to establish and no less difficult to maintain, not only survived and eventually flourished, but also over the years made some impressive contributions to education by promoting the exchange of ideas and serving as a unifying influence in educational development in this country.

If heaven is for people whose reach exceeds their grasp, it should perhaps have more than its share of educationists. As early as October, 1867, a letter was read at the convention of the Provincial Association of Protestant Teachers of Lower Canada from the Provincial Association of Ontario proposing the establishment of an educational organization for the whole Dominion. In consequence, a resolution was adopted that a committee be formed to mature a plan to provide a liaison among the various education associations within the Dominion of Canada. At the Provincial Association of Protestant Teachers convention in Richmond, Quebec, a year later, no progress could be reported, and the committee was continued for another year. In 1869, it was reported at the Protestant teachers' Waterloo convention that it was unlikely that such an organization as a Dominion Educational Association could be formed for some years to come.

Twenty years passed before this proposal came forward again. At that time the proposal took the form of an address by Dr. A. J. Eaton of McGill University, on the subject of a *Dominion Conference of Teachers,* at a convention of the Provincial Association of Protestant Teachers at McGill Normal School in October, 1889. The executive decided to take action on the suggestions contained in this address.

As a result of correspondence which was initiated by Mr. E. W. Arthy, secretary of the executive committee of the Provincial Association of Protestant Teachers, Mr. Arthy was able, in 1890, to report to the Quebec Association: that Mr. U. E. Archambault, Superintendent of Roman Catholic Schools of Montreal, believed Roman Catholic teachers would join such a body; that the Honorable G. W. Ross, Minister of Education, Ontario, favored it if it were undenominational; that Superintendent William Crocket, Fredericton, did not think it was possible; and that Principals A. Anderson of Prince of Wales College, Charlottetown, G. U. Hay of Victoria School, Saint John, and A. McKay of Halifax Academy, Halifax, sympathized with the idea but pointed out that travelling expenses might be prohibitive.

The Quebec Association then adopted the following resolution:

> That whereas at a meeting of our Association, held in August, 1869, in the village of Waterloo, province of Quebec, a committee previously appointed, with Dr. S. P. Robins as chairman, to consider steps to be taken relative to the formation of a teachers' association for British North America, had the matter under consideration, and conferred with provincial associations for the purpose, and reported that there was not then such co-operation as

warranted proceeding further at the time; and whereas this Association has never fully lost sight of such a scheme, which received a fresh impetus at our convention last year through Dr. Eaton's paper before the Association; and whereas a committee was appointed to take steps in the matter; and whereas said committee took immediate steps to bring the matter before the favorable notice of the different provinces by correspondence with prominent educators in each, and by sending delegates to two Associations, namely, the Reverend Elson I. Rexford, B.A., president of this Association, to the Ontario Association, and Dr. Kelly to the Maritime Provinces; we as an association hereby reaffirm our previous action in relation to the formation of a Dominion Association of Teachers, and hereby instruct our secretary to inform the Ontario Teachers' Association[1] that we have the honor to acknowledge the receipt of the resolution of the Ontario Association,[2] and hereby give our assurances of a hearty cooperation in the formation of a Dominion Teachers' Association.

On July 16, 1891, Canadian teachers in attendance at a convention in Toronto of the National Education Association of the United States, held a meeting in the Toronto Normal School with Mr. W. MacIntosh, President of the Ontario Teachers' Association in the chair. All departments of educational work in the Dominion were represented at the meeting. A number of prominent educationists spoke in favor of a Dominion Teachers' Association, the Honorable G. W. Ross of Ontario putting forward the strongest plea.

At a meeting held on July 18, the following resolution was adopted, on motion of the Reverend Dr. Nathaniel Burwash of Victoria College, seconded by Dr. George Bryce of Manitoba College:

That in the opinion of the representatives from the different provinces of the Dominion present, it is desirable that an association for the teachers of the Dominion of Canada should be formed to be called The Educational Association of the Dominion of Canada.

[1]Later named the Ontario Educational Association.
[2]Expressing readiness to consider forming an Association.

"The resolution was carried unanimously and with much applause, all agreeing with the view expressed by several of the speakers, that the time for action had come."

A provisional council was appointed with power to add to their number, to consist of the superintendents or acting ministers of the various provinces, the presidents of the universities of the Dominion, the principals of the normal schools or schools engaged in the teaching of pedagogy, the presidents of all existing teachers' associations throughout the Dominion. With regard to the last group, the presidents of each of the different sections of the Ontario Association were to be included.

The council elected the following officers: president, the Honorable G. W. Ross; vice-presidents, the superintendents and acting ministers of education; secretary, the Reverend E. I. Rexford, Montreal; treasurer, Mr. E. W. Arthy, Montreal. Committees were appointed on a constitution and a program, and an executive was named; the executive was given authority to fix the time and place of meeting and to look after entertainment and transportation.

This, then, was how the Dominion Educational Association was provisionally established in 1891. It was formed as the result of strong efforts of teachers' organizations to unite for the advancement of education. In this undertaking they obtained the support of ministers and superintendents of education, who assumed responsibility for the organization, an arrangement that the teachers of that period both favored and took for granted.

Chapter 2

THE DEA AS A GENERAL EDUCATION
ASSOCIATION, 1892 - 1913

The first convention of the DEA was held in the High School Buildings, Montreal, July 5–8, 1892. The minutes, addresses, papers, and discussions, were published in 1893 in an impressive cloth-bound book of 302 pages, including an index and a list of members. In May, 1892, *The Educational Record,* journal of the Quebec Department of Education (Protestant), forecast and supported the convention by saying: "We have still to keep before our readers the approaching convention to be held in connection with the newly formed Dominion Association of Teachers (sic)." The writer went on to prophesy that "beneath the glare and glitter and evanescent gratulation of a first convention there will be found a kernel of good from which shall spring an organization that has for its object the advancement of the teacher."

Much was expected, undoubtedly too much, from the establishment of the new organization. There was strong support from Quebec, according to *The Educational Record,* which reported on preparations for the convention in the same issue.

> The Roman Catholic and Protestant Committees of the Council of Public Instruction of the Province of Quebec at a recent meeting heartily endorsed the movement, and a deputation from both committees waited upon the government in favor of a grant in aid of the funds of the Association. The Association will meet with the cordial support of all sections of this province, and we shall have the unique spectacle of all sections of our Dominion's population, Roman Catholic and Protestant, French and English, from one end of the Dominion to

the other, meeting together in friendly discussion of the best methods of promoting educational progress in the several provinces of the Dominion. This itself is sufficient to command the hearty support of every true Canadian.

The convention opened with an address of welcome by Sir William Dawson, Principal of McGill University, followed by addresses of welcome from other educational leaders in the province, including representatives of the Roman Catholic and Protestant teachers. Replies were made by the president, by the superintendents of education of Nova Scotia and of New Brunswick, and by the president of the Ontario Teachers' Association.

On the second day, July 6, there was a report on the first draft of the constitution, which was referred to a committee representing the various provinces of the Dominion. The committee reported on a constitution for the Association, and their recommendations were adopted. On the motion of the Honorable Gédéon Ouimet, Superintendent of Public Instruction, Quebec, seconded by Dr. J. R. Inch, Superintendent of Education for New Brunswick, it was unanimously resolved that the Constitution and By-laws should be translated into French and entered in the minute book in that language, and that the name of the Association in French should be L'Association d'Education du Canada.

The report of the committee on resolutions of the first convention of the DEA in 1892 is of particular interest in revealing what occupied the attention of educationists in convention sixty-four years ago. Appreciation was recorded of university extension work; regret was expressed that it should seem necessary for universities to give instruction in secondary school work—the universities should "devote their energies to the higher departments of culture," and the universities should "agree to adopt a common standard of matriculation." Other resolutions dealt with the overlapping of the work of elementary and high schools, the importance of thorough inspection of public and high schools, and the need for uniform nomenclature from province to province in designating schools. The prevalence of truancy and irregular school attendance was deplored, and it was suggested that laws relating to these be made more exacting. It was further believed that more adequate facilities should be provided for teacher-training and that kindergartens should be established as part of the school system in all provinces.

Two resolutions were passed which still receive the attention of delegates to CEA conventions. One concerned the attainment of pupils who transferred from one province to another. The other stated that "the time has arrived when an effort should be made by the various provinces to assimilate the requirements for teachers' certificates and to provide for recognition of them throughout the Dominion." Both of these resolutions, since they involved important policy, were referred to a committee of the ministers and superintendents of the various provinces.

Still another problem occupied the deliberations of that first DEA convention in 1892—a history of the Dominion of Canada. Mr. J. H. Burland of Montreal had offered "a considerable sum of money" as a loan for the preparation of a history on condition that such history should be authorized in at least five of the seven provinces of the Dominion. This, it was felt, would unify the provinces and foster a spirit of patriotism. These highly desirable aims appealed to educationists, supported by the undoubted fact that a uniform text would be much cheaper for pupils because of its production in greater quantities. In spite of these advantages, however, the provisionally organized DEA exhibited from the beginning that discretion which was to become one of its distinguishing characteristics. It was felt that Mr. Burland's offer would involve "personal obligation and responsibility which might ultimately prove embarrassing." In addition, the Royal Society in May thought that no author would undertake the work under the conditions required. It was therefore agreed to advertise that a committee of the DEA would be willing to receive manuscripts of a Dominion history, the initial expense of the history to be borne by the education department of each province, in proportion to the number of its schools, providing its assent was first obtained. The successful competitor would receive 10 per cent royalty on the retail price and the unsuccessful competitors $200 if their manuscripts had merit. The retail price of the book should not exceed 50 cents.

The outcome of this proposal of 1892 is not revealed in the records for some time, but Dr. A. H. MacKay referred to it at the tenth convention in 1918. In an address entitled *Uniform Textbooks for Canadian Schools,* he said that in 1893 every province contributed to a total amount of $2000 for prizes. Forty-six candidates were accepted as qualified to write, and the competition closed on July 1, 1895, with the receipt of fifteen manuscripts. "The first prize was won by Mr. Clements of Toronto, and in 1897 that book was published, after being adopted by several provinces." However, in a few years the book was regarded as out-of-date and discontinued. In Dr. MacKay's opinion the efforts of the DEA had not been altogether successful.

An interesting sidelight on the efforts to implement the very difficult proposal of 1892 is contained in the proceedings of the Provincial Association of Protestant Teachers which, in 1893, reported that it had appointed a committee to aid the DEA in obtaining money towards the production of a textbook in Canadian history. This committee "was assured by the premier of Quebec that Quebec would do its duty, and that the amount would be put in the next estimates."

In the light of the impressive inauguration of the DEA, as revealed in the records of its first convention, much might have been expected of the second convention, held in Toronto on April 16, 17, and 18, 1895, in conjunction with the thirty-fourth annual convention of the Ontario Educational Association. One searches in vain, however, in the joint proceedings of the DEA and the Ontario Educational Association, numbering 408 pages, for developments on the DEA proposals of 1892. Unfortunately, it is difficult to distinguish the DEA from the OEA proceedings, so lost was each in sectionalism of activity and in the exchange of compliments and felicitations.

Considering the records, or lack of them, of the 1895 convention, one wonders if the observations contained in *The Educational Record,* August-September 1892, about the first convention were not both penetrating and well-founded. After stating that the convention was largely organized by the Ontario Minister of Education, the writer assessed the first DEA convention as follows:

The meetings were not very largely attended, except where the gatherings were miscellaneous, such as meetings during the evenings, when large numbers of the citizens of Montreal came out to hear those who had addresses to deliver. The verdict of those who attended the meetings, in regard to the benefits to be derived from such a gathering, was by no means unanimous, yet there were many practical questions touched upon in the discussions . . . which if properly followed up by the executive cannot but realize very beneficial results to the Dominion. Some of the older teachers present were not a little amused at the too evident endeavors that had been made to 'boom' the enterprise, while exception has been taken to the manner in which all matters pertaining to the organization of the Association itself were hurried through by the provisional committee. . . . when the management of its affairs comes to fall out of the hands of officialism into the hands of the teachers of the country, the results of its occasional conventions, we believe, will assume more and more of the practical, and less of the immodest booming which the honest reformer is ever ready to denounce even at the inception of an enterprise that promises to be a good in the land.

Certainly the second DEA convention gave no evidence of progress over the first. The OEA secretary, Mr. R. W. Doan, on behalf of the OEA and DEA, exchanged greetings by cablegram with the National Union of Teachers of England and Wales. Addresses were delivered by the Honorable James Baker of British Columbia on *The Diagnosis of Brain Power,* by Dr. J. M. Harper of Quebec on *Some Pedagogic Fallacies,* and by Mr. G. J. Oulton of Dorchester, New Brunswick, on *The Brotherhood of Teachers.*

Dr. A. H. MacKay, in speaking on behalf of Nova Scotia, remarked, "We are especially proud of Ontario's Minister of Education, and the whole Dominion of Canada owes a great deal to him for his initiative in forming the Dominion Educational Association." Mr. E. I. Rexford, a moving spirit at the 1892 convention, was not at this convention, which probably accounts for the fact that the OEA secretary presumably served also as the DEA secretary. No report is given of an election, but the new officers of the Association are listed at the beginning of the joint proceedings.

If some confusion prevails in the records of the joint meeting of the OEA and the DEA in 1895 as to the progress of the DEA, there is compensation in the proceedings of the third DEA meeting at Halifax in 1898. These, printed in 1900, are contained in a splendidly bound volume of 363 pages, plus 88 pages of introduction.

A change is provided in the Constitution which defines for the first time how often the Association must meet—not more than three years should intervene between two general meetings or conventions.

While there was no reference to the resolutions passed in 1892 (none was reported for the meeting of 1895), several resolutions of considerable importance received endorsement at the 1898 convention.

Among these were recommendations that universities and colleges provide for the teaching of pedagogy, that a committee consider and report upon the establishment of a central bureau of education for Canada, long to be a recurrent theme at DEA meetings, and that the school day immediately preceding May 24 be set aside as "Empire Day" and suitable exercises be held on that occasion. It was further resolved that teachers be engaged for character, manners, and competence rather than on considerations of low salaries.

In his remarks as president, Dr. A. H. MacKay pointed out that four provinces paid the cost of publishing the first proceedings (Ontario $500, Quebec $500, Nova Scotia $200, Manitoba $100 —and the city of Montreal $500), and that now nearly every province, as well as the Northwest Territories, contributed. He referred to the Honorable G. W. Ross as "the father of the DEA." A letter from Mr. Ross, who was at the opening of a new parliament, said that all provinces had approved in correspondence with him the setting aside of a school day for the observance of patriotic exercises and that all that now remained was for the Association to fix the time for observing such a day, and to select a title. This was provided for in the resolution noted above.

It was at this convention that Dr. J. M. Harper, Inspector of High Schools for Quebec (Protestant), gave an address on the

subject of *A National or Central Bureau of Education for Canada.*
Couched in fairly general terms with reference to Canada, much
of the address was devoted to an exposition of the usefulness of
the United States Bureau of Education at Washington.[1]

Attendance at the convention was reported as exceptionally
large, although the number is not given. However, an appendix
lists the membership (including several wives), and this shows an
impressive total of 746. Of these, 91 are from New Brunswick,
11 from Ontario, 10 from Quebec, 3 from Prince Edward Island,
2 from the Northwest Territories, 2 from New York, and one each
from Connecticut and Ohio. The remaining 625 are from Nova
Scotia.

When the fourth convention met in Ottawa in 1901, a preface
to the proceedings expressed regret that attendance at the convention was considerably less than at previous meetings because of
a somewhat smaller reduction in railway rates than had been
expected and because the date was apparently unsuitable to "many
intending delegates."

Further to discussions at the third convention of the need for
a central bureau of education, an oral report was presented on
behalf of the committee by Mr. G. U. Hay. No information is
given as to the nature of the report. That it was inconclusive may
be assumed from the fact that the committee was instructed to
continue and to report at the next meeting.

A committee had also been appointed in 1898 to report upon:
1. the universal use of the decimal system of weights and
   measures;
2. the simplification of English orthography;
3. the general introduction of a distinctly legible phonetic short-
   hand.

It is suggestive of the casual nature of the organization of the
DEA that no member of the committee was present; the matters
under the committee's consideration were consequently postponed
to the next convention.

Among the resolutions was one endorsing efforts to remove
illiteracy among laboring groups in newer districts in Canada

[1]See Chapters 7 and 11.

through elementary instruction and travelling libraries. A second significant one established a senior committee consisting of Dr. D. J. Goggin, Superintendent, Northwest Territories, Dr. MacKay, Nova Scotia Superintendent, the Honorable Boucher de la Bruère, Quebec Superintendent, and the Honorable Richard Harcourt, Ontario Minister of Education, to study the matter of a Dominion registration of teachers. The latter resolution, related to the possible interprovincial recognition of teachers' certificates, still occupies some attention at meetings of the CEA and of the Canadian Teachers' Federation. The desirability of a Dominion registration of trained teachers was the subject of an address at this convention by Dr. S. P. Robins, Principal of McGill Normal School.

One of the most significant addresses yet to be delivered to the DEA, in the light of its later history and, indeed, in the light of interprovincial developments in education, was one by Dr. J. M. Harper. This address dealt much more specifically with the subject of *An Educational Bureau for the Dominion of Canada* than did his address to the DEA in 1898. Dr. Harper urged that such a bureau be established by the federal government along the lines of the Bureau of Education in the United States. He revealed that a deputation from the committee appointed at the last convention had interviewed Sir Wilfrid Laurier, the Prime Minister, on this matter and that Sir Wilfrid had "promised to look into the whole question."

The Honorable Boucher de la Bruère made a formal reply to Dr. Harper's proposal, expressing regret that attempts should be made to have it adopted. He stated that the Catholic committee had considered the idea in May, 1899. In consequence, the committee had adopted a resolution that the establishment of a federal department was neither constitutional nor desirable. Dr. de la Bruère went on to say that "there is no ambiguity in the above resolution and there can be no misconception with regard to the opinion so clearly expressed by the Committee of the Council of Public Instruction which in our province represents the great majority of the population."

The Superintendent described the work of the Bureau in Washington and elaborated on the reasons why such a federal office in Ottawa, or one somewhat similar to it, would be un-acceptable to the province of Quebec.[1]

When the fifth convention of the DEA met in Winnipeg, July 26–29, 1904, it was proposed that the convention be held, if at all possible, every two years rather than every three years.

As at the last meeting, efforts to provide education in frontier, railway construction, and lumbering areas were commended. Reso-lutions urged better moral instruction in the schools, more generous financial aid for education, and greater emphasis upon patriotism. A committee was appointed to collect statistics on teachers' salaries.

The records make it possible to compare the membership at the time of the Winnipeg convention in 1904 with that at the Halifax convention in 1898. Distance appears to have been a determining factor, for the membership, according to the records, was as follows (several figures from the 1898 meeting are shown in brackets): British Columbia, 5 (0); Manitoba, 240 (0); New Brunswick, 1 (91); Northwest Territories, 39; Nova Scotia, 5 (625); Ontario, 63 (11); Quebec, 5; England, 2; United States, 1 —a total of 361.

There were no significant resolutions but many addresses at the sixth convention in Toronto in 1907. The minutes, having been published as usual, were, as usual, taken as read, and it was agreed that the next meeting be held in Victoria, British Columbia, in 1909. New officers were elected and the convention adjourned after passing several routine resolutions of thanks.

It is worthy of note that the Honorable R. A. Pyne, Ontario Minister of Education, in his welcoming address, stressed the im-portance of industrial and agricultural education; Dr. David Soloan, Principal of the Truro Normal School, spoke on behalf of Dr. A. H. MacKay who was absent in Europe studying technical edu-cation which was soon to be inaugurated in Nova Scotia. Addresses on these aspects of education were shortly to occupy considerable attention at DEA meetings.

It should be noted, too, that French-speaking Quebec, though represented at previous conventions, was not represented in 1904 in Winnipeg nor indeed again until 1917.

[1]See Chapter 7.

Brisker and better organized than any since 1898, the 1909 convention in Victoria opened on Tuesday afternoon, July 13, with two addresses of welcome and five replies, as it was customary to have several replies to the welcomes. On Tuesday evening there was a government reception in the form of a band concert, promenade, and refreshments, and on July 14 the convention settled down to a round table discussion of proposals for making the DEA a more influential factor in Canadian education.

These proposals of 1909 are so relevant to developments in the CEA some thirty-six years later that they are quoted here in full.

1. Appointment of a permanent secretary at a fixed salary, devoting, if possible, his whole time to the work.
2. Systematic effort to enrol every teacher in the Dominion, and every other person vitally interested in education, as permanent members of the DEA.
3. The holding of a convention at least once in two years.
4. A special committee to be appointed to prepare convention programs for every department of the DEA, the chairman of the committee and a majority of the members to be within easy reach of the place where the convention is to meet. The President of the Association, the General Secretary, and the chairman of each section, to be *ex-officio* members of such committee.
5. Each provincial government to send at least one special representative to every convention, and to pay the expenses of the same.
6. Effort to keep members fully informed re educational affairs at home and abroad:
   (*a*) Publication in book form of full report of proceedings and addresses at conventions of the DEA.
   (*b*) Publication of an annual report summarizing condition of progress of educational affairs in each province.
   (*c*) Publication of a high-class education monthly or quarterly, discussing national problems of education from a national point of view.
   (*d*) The Secretary of the Association to be editor-in-chief of publications.

7. Increased revenue to be derived as follows:
   (a) Annual fees from increased membership.
   (b) Increased provincial grants to be paid annually.
8. Strong and united effort to induce the Dominion government to establish a bureau of education at Ottawa, similar to the bureau of education at Washington.
9. Changes in the constitution of the DEA in harmony with the foregoing proposals.
10. Appointment of a representative committee at the Victoria meeting to assist in carrying out the suggestions approved, and to report progress at the next meeting of the Association.

The discussion on the proposals was led by Mr. T. A. Brough of the high school staff, Vancouver. Mr. Brough paid tribute to the foresight of the men who had founded the DEA, but he felt that the progress expected had not been made. Since the organization lacked continuity and persistence, useful proposals had been made but never pursued. In Mr. Brough's view:

> The crux of the whole situation seems to me to lie in the appointment of a permanent secretary. We have the work of the secretary done this year in an admirable manner. He has kept the Association affairs running along smoothly; he has got acquainted with the railway magnates who fix the rates; he has corresponded with the ministers and deputies and the superintendents of education throughout the Dominion; he has come into contact with the principals and professors of universities; he has been brought into communication with the great leaders of educational thought on the other side of the line and across the Atlantic; and just when he is becoming extremely valuable to us and to the educational work of Canada, there is a chance of our losing his services. Now, would any good business undertaking, any great corporation, do business like that; appoint an untried man to a responsible position and then when he made good, won golden opinions, consent to be deprived of his services and have to begin all over again with a new man? I need not ask you; the question answers itself. We ought, then, to have a permanent secretary for this Association. He would keep us at work along certain lines. He would see that when we began a good work we would make some effort

to finish the work begun. He would be acquainted with the leaders of educational thought in every part of the country and he could easily interest them in our work. If he could not get their services to come to the convention one year he could another year. He would be our managing director.

Mr. Brough stressed the need for a larger and more permanent membership, a more active interest by the departments of education in the DEA, with representative attendance at each convention, an educational magazine, and an educational bureau at Ottawa.

The views put forward by Mr. Brough were supported in part by Professor A. E. Lang of Victoria University, Toronto. He thought that "we are now in a position, if never before, to make a move of vital importance not only to the Association as a whole, but for the educational interests of the country at large." He did not believe that the Association secretary should also be required to edit a quarterly magazine; the latter should be edited by other persons. "The wise plan for the Association to pursue would be to pay the secretary a handsome salary and let him devote all his time to further the interests of the Association. It might be possible to secure the services of a man or group of men to conduct the magazine and pay contributors."

Professor Lang did not think that it would be possible for a bureau of education to be established at Ottawa, much as he himself favored the suggestion. In view of the dissension such a bureau would cause, he thought it would be better for a bureau to be established in connection with the DEA itself.

Dr. W. A. McIntyre of the Winnipeg Normal School sent his views on the future of the DEA in a letter. He pointed out that the Association could only hope to find at its meetings a large local representation and comparatively few delegates from outside the province. He thought that the organization needed a permanent secretary, but more important was a federal bureau at Ottawa. Should this be established, an official of the bureau could act as secretary of the Association. Dr. McIntyre further believed that "if the Dominion authorities should refuse to accede to a reasonable request, it would be the highest wisdom on the part of the provinces to combine in supporting a bureau of this kind."

Dr. A. H. MacKay, long one of the most active supporters of the DEA, thought that there ought to be a federal bureau of education. If there could not, then there should be representative meetings through the DEA, and also a bureau at Ottawa for the collection of statistics. This alternative proposal by Dr. MacKay accurately forecast the two developments which have subsequently taken place.

Mr. D. S. MacKenzie, Deputy Minister, Alberta, thought that there should be larger membership and continued contacts with leading educationists, which required a general secretary, and that there should be an education bureau either in the hands of the Dominion government, or with the provinces in complete control of it if this were financially possible. Mr. MacKenzie went on to say:

> Some allusion has been made which may be an objection to the former course. The differences of language may, perhaps, be a barrier though I cannot for my own part see why it should be a great barrier. If this Association, however, through its increased membership and increased powers, should be able to control this bureau itself, then it can be made perhaps still more valuable to the educationists of the Dominion and will be of very much more interest to the membership.

Mr. R. Von Munster of Victoria said rather pertinently that he did not see how a general opinion could be obtained from a meeting of 300 British Columbia delegates and a small number from the rest of Canada. Dr. A. Melville Scott, Superintendent of City Schools, Calgary, remarked that he would approve proposals for making the DEA more effective, but to what purpose—who would pay a secretary's salary, for instance?

During the discussion, Mr. Frank Andrews of Victoria High School suggested that the really important matter was the establishment of an education bureau in Ottawa; Mr. J. R. Brown remarked pointedly and not without humor, that if these resolutions were left pending for another two years, "we may as well add another letter to the initials of our Association and write it DEAD. Let us get busy and do something right away now." After further discussion the following resolution was adopted:

That we do now approve in a general way of the suggestions made in the program for making the Dominion Education Association a more influential factor in Canadian education, and that a committee be appointed to report to this convention on Thursday as to which clauses should be included in the resolution of this convention to form the basis of future action.

The committee appointed as a result of this resolution subsequently brought in the following report:

Your committee appointed to consider the suggestions as printed on the convention program, for making the Dominion Educational Association a more influential factor in Canadian education, beg to report as follows:

We find that the carrying out of the suggestions made depends almost entirely on the ability of the Association to secure and pay for the services of a permanent secretary, and we therefore recommend the appointment of a committee of nine members, one from each province, with power to add to their numbers, to consider the whole question in its various aspects, financial and otherwise; to interview the governments of the various provinces and of the Dominion, ascertain whether ways and means can be found to support a permanent secretary, and present a complete report at the next meeting of the Association.

We further recommend that the following constitute the committee: Professor J. W. Robertson, Quebec; W. P. Argue, British Columbia; Dr. A. M. Scott, Alberta; Dr. W. C. Murray, Saskatchewan; Dr. W. A. McIntyre, Manitoba; Professor W. S. Milner, Ontario; Dr. W. Hamilton, New Brunswick; Dr. D. Soloan, Nova Scotia; Principal S. Robertson, Prince Edward Island.

The report of the committee was adopted. A further resolution was passed that if the committee considering the future of the DEA after consulting with the executive, thought that a conference should be held in 1910, the authority was granted.

The development in thinking on the function and the potentialities of the DEA as an organization reached a peak at the Victoria convention in 1909 which it did not again attain until 1942. Undoubtedly Mr. Von Munster's remark quoted above recognized the fact that the DEA as yet lacked any deep support throughout Canada. The officials concerned felt academically that the organization was needed, but they had no strong conviction that they as individuals ought personally to do anything about it.

Confirmation of this opinion is available from the directors' minutes, written in longhand, which are fortunately available for this period. There were only five at the pre-convention meeting, President Alexander Robinson, A. M. Scott of Calgary, W. P. Argue, T. A. Brough, A. C. Stewart of Vancouver, and the secretary, J. D. Buchanan. With regard to the directors' meeting following the convention, it is reported that it was impracticable to hold the meeting planned for July 16, and an informal meeting of the directors still in Victoria was held on the morning of July 17. It is not recorded which or how many directors were present. The directors at this informal meeting following the momentous discussions at the convention confined themselves to approving the payment of convention bills and appointing Mr. S. W. Matthews, Principal of the High School, Vancouver, as auditor; they then adjourned. Seldom has so much discussion led to so little action. As it turned out, the brief minutes of that meeting were not considered or approved until the next directors' meeting on August 20, 1913.

Although it was planned that the DEA would meet in 1911, so many DEA members and representatives were in Europe that summer and again in 1912, that the meeting was further delayed. An additional reason for the postponement of the convention until the summer of 1913 was that it would permit DEA members to give full consideration to a forthcoming report of a Royal Commission on Industrial and Technical Education.

Chapter 3

THE DEA BECOMES REPRESENTATIVE
AND STATIC, 1913 - 1934

The chief subject of the eighth convention in Ottawa, August 20–23, 1913, was not the future of the Association which occupied so much attention in 1909, but the report of the Royal Commission on Industrial Training and Technical Education, a summary of which was available to the delegates. The DEA president, Dr. J. W. Robertson of Ottawa, who was a member of the Commission, devoted his address to its procedures and recommendations.

It was left to Dr. A. H. MacKay, so often a spokesman in this matter, to continue to press for some co-ordinating agency in Canadian education. He took as the topic of his address, *Are There Any Advantageous Co-ordinations Practicable Between the Educational Systems of the Provinces?* Dr. MacKay recommended four measures: (1) community of textbooks; (2) uniform standards for matriculation and professional training; (3) a Dominion Education Bureau similar to that at Washington; and (4) development of the Dominion Educational Association into a body of representative and advisory character rather than a general association.

With reference to his third suggestion, Dr. MacKay pointed out that all the education departments in the Empire were then outlining their education systems for the education department at London, England, but that there was no centre in Canada which could prepare a report on "general progress in educational legislation and statistics in the Dominion as a whole." He felt there should be a central bureau in Canada for this purpose.

Dr. MacKay's fourth proposal was very significant for the eventual development of the DEA. He thought that "it should become of a more representative, co-ordinating, and advisory character" rather than a "generalized provincial educational association." Under present arrangements, the only successful meetings were those held when the DEA combined its meeting with that of a provincial association. Dr. MacKay therefore believed that the DEA meetings should be primarily for representatives from each province, "including *ex-officio* representatives from each education department," who would meet annually. This view was supported by Dr. W. S. Carter, Superintendent of Education for New Brunswick.

Following some discussion, the president, Dr. J. W. Robertson, stated that:

> . . . the present meeting would be satisfactory, if nothing else should come from it but the beginnings of action whereby the superintendents of education and a few other responsible men should get together once a year to talk over the standards in the provinces and practicable co-ordinations for the progress of education in the Dominion as a whole. Every province would contribute to all the rest of the provinces something really worthwhile. Each of the provinces would thus get great good from the others.

Note was made at the conference of the constitutional requirement that not more than three years should intervene between two conferences. Having regard to the long interval since the last meeting (four years), it was agreed, on the recommendation of the directors, that the present meeting should be a regular meeting.

Two resolutions were passed relating to the development of the DEA. The first, proposed by a committee summarizing the discussion introduced by Dr. MacKay, stated "that we view with great satisfaction the disposition on the part of the provincial educational authorities to co-operate . . . in making the Dominion Educational, or some other Association, an efficient bond of interprovincial comity and conference;" the second came forward from a meeting of the Board of Directors and resolved "that this Board, convinced of the necessity of the appointment of a permanent secretary to maintain the continuity of the work of the Association between conventions, suggests that the Association instruct the incoming Board to consider the question and take such action as seems possible to carry it out."

Having regard to the vain hope that this latter resolution was to be for many years, another resolution was more significant in anticipating a necessary prelude to a secretariat. This was:

> That the Dominion Educational Association, being convinced of the very great advantage to be gained by each of the provinces through regular meetings between representatives of the education departments of the several provinces, instructs the President (Dr. J. W. Robertson) to suggest to the Inter-Provincial Conference[1] the advisability of arranging for the holding of an annual conference of deputy ministers and superintendents of education (or their representatives).

The ninth convention held in Ottawa on January 31 and February 1 and 2, 1917, was the first to be held in mid-winter, and it was notable for the attendance of the Honorable Cyrille Delâge,[2] Superintendent of Education, Quebec. Catholic Quebec had not been represented at DEA meetings since 1901. A feature of the convention, no doubt arising from the proposals of the convention of 1913, was that each department of education was represented by an official delegate who was so named. A list of members who registered contains only thirty-one names, but, including inspectors, they held positions of considerable influence.

A round table discussion was held on the subject of a federal bureau of education; this was again introduced by Dr. A. H. MacKay. On this occasion he laid emphasis on the collection of educational statistics. He noted that some small beginning had been made in the last *Canada Year Book* and he felt that the DEA should commend this action and encourage more of it.

In support of some sort of central office, Dr. J. F. White referred to the need for training children to have many things in common. Dr. White regretted that "education is rather parochial, rather local, than even provincial or nation-wide." He spoke of the influx of foreigners which would follow the conclusion of the war and who would need to be instructed in Canadian ideals.

---

[1]A meeting of provincial premiers in Ottawa.
[2]So named in the records, but not actually a cabinet minister.

Dr. H. L. Brittain delivered an address on the need for *A National Clearing House for Education*. He put forward the same view as that given at previous conventions "that no centre of Canadian educational thought and activity is having so much effect, directly and indirectly, on the Canadian educational consciousness as the publications of the United States Bureau." His suggestion was that "some Canadian millionaire, preferably one who has made some of his money in munitions," should provide an educational fund to establish a national clearing house in education which could be administered by the provincial departments of education and the provincial and Dominion educational associations. Failing this, there should at least be a national educational magazine for the publication of educational information and to serve as a forum for discussion.

Dr. Brittain stated that the three functions of a national bureau of education were:

1. for the study of educational reports, magazines, and general literature; for the digesting of these, and making the information available to education authorities and students;
2. to act as a clearing house of information for educational authorities and teachers;
3. to make field studies of educational experiments and tests at the invitation of provincial authorities.

Mr. Delâge, representing Quebec, said that the proposal for a national office was interesting but not new. Since he had been asked to express an opinion on a federal bureau of education, he was glad to do so. Pointing out that this suggestion had arisen in Halifax in 1897[1] and in Ottawa in 1901, he said that the Catholic Committee in Quebec had expressed its views in May, 1899. The reasons against such a bureau still existed, and he could see no reason for concurring in its creation. As for statistics, the federal government already had power to collect these, and Quebec would co-operate within this just purpose.

The representative from Ontario, Dr. John Waugh, Chief Inspector of Schools, remarked, as perhaps has often been remarked in the CEA, "I sympathize with the position taken by the

[1]The Halifax meeting was in 1898, not 1897.

Minister of Education of Quebec (*sic*), and so long as there is divided counsel among us in this matter, I think we should not press the matter."[1] Thus once again the idea of a federal office was suppressed, and the DEA was forced to look within itself for methods of educational contact and liaison.

As a result of a lengthy discussion of the future of the Association, it was felt that:

1. Ottawa was the best place to meet;
2. the meeting should be representative;
3. the deputy ministers should meet at least once a year;
4. the Association should separate itself from meetings of local associations and carry on its own programs.

A committee appointed to consider the future of the Association brought forward a resolution which was seconded by Mr. Delâge and carried.

> BE IT RESOLVED that the Dominion Educational Association consist of representatives of provincial Departments of Education, representatives of school inspection and supervision and other phases of school administration, representatives of associations of trustees, and representatives of normal schools and university departments of education.
>
> That the Dominion Educational Association be reorganized on the basis of a Dominion council, and that the Board of Directors be instructed to determine a basis of representative organization of these constituent factors and to publish their findings instead of the present constitution.

At this convention Dr. J. W. Robertson gave a luncheon at the Rideau Club so that the senior members of the DEA might consult with Sir George Foster regarding a Dominion bureau for educational statistics. Sir George expressed interest and said that he would have the Dominion statistician, Mr. R. H. Coats, discuss the matter with representatives from each of the provinces. A memorandum on the preparation of such statistics by the Dominion Bureau of Statistics, prepared by Mr. Coats, was given to Dr. A. H. MacKay to circulate to these representatives.

[1]See Chapter 7.

A new constitution was adopted on November 21, 1918, at the tenth convention in Ottawa, providing a new name for the Association—Canadian Education Association—and a different type of organization.

Although DEA officers discussed with federal officials at the 1917 convention the pressing need for the collection of educational statistics, the substantial part played by the CEA in the establishment of the Education Division of the Dominion Bureau of Statistics is mentioned only inconspicuously in the 1918 proceedings. The president, Dr. W. S. Carter, said that the Association was asked if it would approve, in the form of a resolution, the collection of educational statistics. If so, the Bureau would appoint some person competent in education to file such statistics. In consequence, the CEA recorded "its appreciation of the action of the Honorable Sir George Foster in gathering and publishing statistics" and approved "the appointment of an expert educationist to the department in Ottawa."

The eleventh convention was also held in Ottawa, but not until November 1, 1922, four years after the tenth. In welcoming the delegates, the president, Dr. F. W. Merchant, explained the reason for this, and in doing so implicitly revealed that the CEA after thirty years was still haphazard in organization and hardly commanded impressive attention. As explained by the president, the occasion of the present meeting was a gathering, in Toronto, of the ministers of education of the different provinces and of officials representing the departments of education. The meeting having concluded in Toronto, many of the officials found it convenient to come to Ottawa. In the interval since the last convention, a National Conference on Education had met in Winnipeg.[1] A year later, another conference was held in Ottawa, called by the Minister of Labor. It was not thought advisable to duplicate these meetings. "The present occasion is the first in which we have had an open field," the president stated.

The modest position of the CEA at that time is also revealed in a question addressed to the president by Dean Sinclair Laird of Macdonald College during the discussion. Dr. Laird asked if there

[1]See Chapter 8.

would be a meeting of the deputy ministers before the next CEA meeting. The reply was that it was just possible that some action that was taken in Toronto would lead to the assembling of a body representative of the provinces.

At this meeting there was again discussion about the future of the CEA, ably introduced by the president, Dr. G. W. Parmelee, English Secretary to the Quebec Department of Education. Dr. Parmelee pointed out that early meetings of the CEA were held in conjunction with a provincial teachers' association meeting which "pretty well swamped" the CEA. He thought this unsatisfactory. The CEA could not really function as a national meeting of teachers because the teachers present were almost entirely local. Pointing out that the ministers and deputies had met two years previously in Quebec, and immediately before the current meeting, in Toronto, he thought that the CEA ought to occupy an intermediate place between the latter and the teachers' associations. The president thought that the CEA was settling down to be a working body—a small body but a more effective one.

The constitution was amended to provide for biennial meetings on the first Tuesday in November.

The president commented, regarding a question on amending the constitution, "This Association is made up mainly of administrators and heads of schools. The idea was that it not be a general association like the OEA (Ontario Educational Association) or the NEA (National Educational Association) but that it be made up of the people who are controlling education."

Conventions were held successively in Ottawa in 1913, 1917, 1918, and 1922. So, too, was the twelfth convention, November 10–12, 1925, but it is interesting to note that it was, by some curious error, called the thirteenth convention. This error in numbering has since persisted, so that numbers given to successive conventions thereafter have actually been one higher than they should be. The thirteenth convention was undoubtedly the twelfth. It is reported on page 14 of the proceedings of this convention that "the Secretary presented the printed minutes of the 1922 meeting (the eleventh convention) which on motion of Mr. D. A. Campbell were adopted."

Neither the printed CEA proceedings nor the minutes of the directors' meeting refer to this error in the numbering of conventions, even though in the Association it was a practice to refer to a convention by number, the number being printed conspicuously on the cover of the proceedings.

The secretary, Dr. J. H. Putnam, reported that two pamphlets had been printed following the meeting of 1922, one on *Federal Aid to Agriculture* and another on *Conditions Governing the Granting of Teachers' Certificates in the Various Provinces.*

The tide in the affairs of the CEA, never in flood in its first half-century, was at its lowest ebb in the 1920's. Little progress can be discovered in the records of the CEA from 1922 to 1929 inclusive, although two items indicate that the CEA occupied a position of at least some responsibility. At the 1925 convention, Mr. J. C. Sutherland, Inspector of Schools, Quebec, doubted the wisdom of a resolution implying approval of a certain type of map on the grounds that "the different provinces might feel bound to approve of it because of the resolution adopted by this body."

The second instance occurred at the fourteenth convention in Winnipeg, November 1–3, 1927, which devoted considerable attention to technical education. A lengthy resolution urged the government of Canada to extend its financial assistance in this field to the provinces for a further ten years. In the resolution, reference was made to "this Canadian Education Association, representing all the provinces . . ." To what extent this meant in some official sense, however, it is not possible to say.

If reference to the convention proceedings gives no evidence of progress in the 1920's, the minutes of the directors' meetings of that period are equally unrewarding. Between November 22, 1918, and November 10, 1925, there was only one meeting—at noon on Thursday, November 2, 1922. Present were Dr. F. W. Merchant, Mr. J. W. Gibson, Mr. F. Peacock, Mr. R. B. Vaughan, and Dr. J. H. Putnam. Their deliberations occupied a page in longhand, and agreed that the 1924 meeting (not held) be held in Ottawa, that the secretary-treasurer pay expenses for the 1922 meeting, that the provinces be asked for a grant to pay for meeting in 1924, that the secretary publish a pamphlet to aid the provinces in issuing "equivalent certificates," and that the secretary be paid an honor-arium of $400.

Other records of minutes give brief and monotonous instructions to the secretary-treasurer to pay accounts, to write the provinces stressing the urgent need of the Association for regular grants, to print and distribute the proceedings, to determine with the president and certain other directors the place and program of the next convention, and to pay himself an honorarium.

Chapter 4

THE CEA BECOMES ACTIVE, 1934 - 1938

Although its constitution required the Association to meet biennially, the CEA did not meet again until 1934, five years after its last meeting. No reason is recorded for the failure to meet, but it is possible that the lassitude of the twenties, the hope that the National Council of Education would establish a central education office, and the onset of the depression were the major factors. In any event, a convention resolution rebuked the officers for postponing the convention and instructed them in the future to observe the requirements of the constitution.

In the interval, the CEA president, Mr. J. T. Ross, had retired from government office and resigned from the Association; Mr. H. H. Shaw, vice-president, succeeded him. If the printed list of delegates can be relied upon as complete, only sixty-seven persons attended the convention. However, an evening session, in the form of public addresses, was held at Convocation Hall, University of Toronto, at which both Dr. H. J. Cody, President of the University, and Professor T. H. Briggs of Teachers College, Columbia University, spoke.

Of the sixty-seven delegates at the convention, the great majority were from Ontario. The list of those from outside the province is sufficiently short to give their names here. They were Professor Fred Clarke, McGill University; the Honorable Cyrille Delâge, Quebec Superintendent of Education, and Dr. W. P. Percival, one of his deputies; Mr. J. L. Watson, Registrar, British Columbia Department of Education; Mr. G. F. McNally, Superintendent of Schools, Alberta; Dr. H. F. Munro, Nova Scotia

Superintendent of Education, and his Director of Technical Education, Dr. F. H. Sexton; and Dr. H. H. Shaw, Superintendent of Education, Prince Edward Island. However, these were all persons of substantial influence in education, as were the Ontario delegates.

A proposal of considerable significance at this point in CEA affairs was made by Mr. G. F. McNally who suggested the appointment of committees that would attempt to solve certain specific educational problems in which all provinces were interested. "Reports from such committees would give to the convention a purpose and a value which it at present lacks." Mr. McNally's proposal offered a practical procedure for the aim expressed by the president, Mr. H. H. Shaw, in his opening address, when he said:

We aim to foster in all the provinces the same ideals. It is therefore essential that those responsible for the schools in one province should learn the nature and direction of progress in the schools of the other provinces and localities. This is the peculiar function of our Association.

One resolution passed by the convention expressed the growing feeling of educators at that time that there should be a closer relationship between the various educational interests of the provinces of the Dominion, and that this should be fostered by a frequent exchange of opinions wherever possible.

Other resolutions showed the interest of the delegates in using the Association as a means of obtaining information that they felt would be of value to them. Such resolutions were:

Resolution 7. That a committee, to be named by the incoming directors, be authorized to investigate the courses of study in the provinces of the Dominion, with a view to selecting the best elements in each and transmitting the information and recommendations to the several departments of education.

Resolution 8. That a committee, to be named by the incoming directors, be authorized to investigate the conditions required for entrance to the normal schools in the various provinces and the length of professional training required in each.

Resolution 9. That a committee, to be named by the incoming directors, be authorized to investigate the practices and procedures of the various examination systems.

Resolution 12. That the Canadian Education Association [establish] a committee which shall begin immediately to investigate the standards required for graduation from the high schools of the various provinces and for admission to the universities, with a view to providing a course of greater flexibility, which at the same time will admit to the universities.

The proceedings of the 1934 convention devotes a page to a meeting of the Board of Directors at the close of the convention. Those present were Drs. G. F. Rogers, H. F. Munro, and W. P. Percival, Mr. G. F. McNally, and Mr. J. L. Watson (representing Dr. S. J. Willis, British Columbia, Superintendent of Education)— a total of five, and presumably the secretary, Dr. W. J. Karr, although this is not stated. Nine directors were elected that morning, in addition to a president, vice-president, and secretary-treasurer, even though the constitution provided for a past president, vice-president, secretary-treasurer, and twelve directors.

A resolution the directors passed regarding new movements in education was of special significance:

That information concerning new movements in education and changes in educational policy occurring in any province should be communicated to each of the other provinces, and that the various departments be asked by the secretary to forward this information promptly and regularly.

The next convention, held in Regina in 1936, was an important and well-attended one, although the majority of delegates were Saskatchewan educationists. The first session of the convention in those times was devoted to a business meeting, and on this occasion Miss Jessie Norris of Montreal, on behalf of the Canadian Teachers' Federation, indicated the desire of that body to co-operate with the CEA in establishing a bureau of educational research. She moved "that the Canadian Education Association appoint a small committee representative of the various provinces to study the possibility of forming a Dominion Bureau of Educational Research." The motion was seconded and after some favorable discussion carried. A committee was appointed, consisting of Dr. F. M. Quance, Dr. H. C. Newland, Dr. H. B. Spaulding, Dr. A. S. MacFarlane, Mr. W. Saddler, and Miss Jessie Norris, to report at the final session of the convention. At that session, Dr. Quance, Dr. Spaulding, Dr. W. O. Rothney, and Mr. H. P. Moffatt were named as a committee to "confer with the committee of the Canadian Teachers' Federation with regard to the possibility of establishing a Dominion Bureau of Educational Research."[1]

The president, Dr. G. F. Rogers, pointed out that at the last two conventions reports on educational developments in each province had been printed but not given orally. Since he thought that "these reports of progress should constitute one of the main features of the meetings," he proposed that they be heard during the convention.

Following an address by Dr. John E. Robbins, of the Education Branch of the Dominion Bureau of Statistics, there was discussion of the work of the Branch, and it was agreed that the Dominion Bureau of Statistics be regularly invited to send a representative to the CEA meeting. Dr. Robbins referred to the early part that the CEA had played in establishing the Education Branch, quoting the resolutions adopted at the 1918 convention. Action along the lines approved by the CEA in 1918 followed in 1919, and the publication of information on education by the Dominion Bureau of Statistics arose "in no small measure through the instrumentality of the Canadian Education Association." Dr. Robbins gave the CEA an important status in 1936 when he said, "The Bureau recognizes in you the most representative assembly of Canadian educationists." This indication of importance, however, must be tempered with the realization that the CEA did not rank above other agencies, but that it was the *only* agency that could be assumed on occasion to represent the collective opinion of the provincial authorities. Indeed, the Association had gained substantially beween 1934 and 1936, as shown by the fact that, in the interval, each provincial department had made a modest grant to its support. (Ontario and Quebec each paid $400, the other provinces $100.)

It is of no small significance in the development of the CEA that each of the committees appointed at the preceding convention had prepared and made available to the convention substantial

[1]See Chapter 9.

reports on high school graduation requirements, requirements for admission to the normal schools, and provincial examinations. The CEA convention was, as Mr. McNally had proposed in 1934 it should, serving a tangible, useful purpose.

At the last convention before the onset of World War II (Maritimes, 1938), the CEA was still a small, but none the less representative, body. Only fifty-eight delegates are shown as registered, just twice the present number of directors, but among these were many of the most influential figures in Canadian education. Manitoba was not represented at all, nor was the Ontario Deputy Minister present. However, a number of senior Ontario officials attended, as did the deputy ministers of the seven other provinces, including Mr. B. O. Filteau and Dr. W. P. Percival; Mr. L. W. Shaw, Director of Education for Newfoundland, was there. Present also were the Deans of Education of the Ontario College of Education (Dr. J. G. Althouse), the School of Education, University of Saskatchewan (Dr. F. M. Quance), and the School of Education, University of Alberta (Dr. M. E. LaZerte). This convention was held in conjunction with a meeting of the Canadian Association for Adult Education and the Canadian Handicrafts Guild.

It was reported that a meeting of the Board of Directors had been held in Toronto on April 18, 1938, consisting of Dr. H. F. Munro, Dr. W. P. Percival, Dr. G. F. Rogers, Mr. V. K. Greer, and the Secretary, Dr. Althouse. Two matters had occupied the directors' attention, one the place and program of the present convention—the latter being left to the president and secretary—the other a discussion of the establishment of a Dominion Bureau of Educational Research. It had been proposed that a committee, as widely representative of the Dominion as possible, be selected by the president and the secretary to formulate a plan for the Bureau for discussion at the 1938 convention, and that the Carnegie Corporation be asked for a grant to cover the cost of the meeting of this committee. The committee had met on May 30, 1938, in Toronto, and it provided the delegates with a report.

A resolution was adopted that a Canadian Council for Educational Research be established,[1] and it was suggested that the

[1]See Chapter 9.

nominations committee nominate the first council. However, it was decided that, since the CEA had assumed responsibility for establishing the council, the question of its support and organization should be left to the CEA directors. This reliance of the membership upon the directors to plan and implement the details of some general resolution was significant of their growing interest and authority.

Several resolutions were passed which indicated the increasing use of the CEA as an instrument for co-operative action. One instructed the executives to seek removal of customs duties on educational tests and scales; another resolved to ask the Postmaster-General for a reduction in postal rates for library books; a third asked the president to "appoint a committee to enquire into all textbooks connected with the courses of study in each of the provinces of the Dominion, with a view to fostering the best ideals of national life, and enquiring closely into their costs."

An event of particular significance at this convention was the desire expressed by Newfoundland, through Dr. L. W. Shaw, Secretary of Education for Newfoundland, to become associated with the Canadian provinces in the CEA. This desire was viewed with gratification, and the constitution amended to permit it; the name of the Association was changed to The Canada and Newfoundland Education Association.

A meeting of the directors was held upon the conclusion of the convention, and it was tentatively decided to hold the next convention in Victoria in 1940. It is particularly worthy of note that it was agreed to have a standing executive committee which would meet from time to time as required, especially for planning the convention; composition of this committee was determined as the centrally-located directors, together with the president, past president, and the secretary-treasurer. No provision existed in the constitution at that time for such an executive.

At the directors' meeting, it was resolved that Dr. J. G. Althouse be "elected and duly installed as secretary-treasurer," although he had also been so elected by the general convention that afternoon. It is possible that this seemingly unnecessary motion reflected the feeling of the directors that concrete action between conventions was now expected of them, and that they looked to the new secretary-treasurer to assume major responsibility in initiating it.

Mention should be made of the impressive migrations of the 1938 convention, subsequently described by one director[1] as the "Peripatetic Convention." With a vigor and an adaptability not previously, nor again, shown by the CEA, the delegates met in Halifax on August 15 and 16, in Saint John on August 17 (evening) and 18, and in Charlottetown on August 19, all day and in the evening. Nor was even this schedule, accompanied by the transaction of considerable important business, arduous enough; the delegates further distinguished themselves by pausing, en route from Saint John to Charlottetown, at Sackville, where they were present as guests at the summer convocation of Mount Allison University and at a tea following the convocation.

[1]Dr. J. G. Althouse.

Chapter 5

THE WAR BRINGS RESPONSIBILITIES,
1941 - 1945

At the 1938 convention, it had been tentatively agreed to meet in 1940 in Victoria. War intervened, and the CNEA met instead in Ottawa in 1941. This was the first convention after the onset of war, and the principal topics, other than proposals for the expansion of the CNEA itself so that it might be of greater service, were education for citizenship, appreciation of democracy, and the re-establishment of veterans following the war.

At the 1941 convention, for the first time since the CNEA had become a representative organization, the delegates divided themselves into various panels for purposes of group discussion. Reports from the groups were later presented and discussed. Subsequently, general approval was given to this feature of the convention program, with the suggestion that it be continued in the future.

A detailed report was received from the Canadian Council for Educational Research,[1] and the constitution was amended to provide for annual, instead of biennial, meetings. Among resolutions passed was one urging the incoming executive to attempt to obtain funds to cover the salary of a permanent secretary and, if such funds were available, to employ a full-time secretary.

> Owing to the expanding interest in education in Canada and Newfoundland and the resulting demands made upon this Association,
>
> BE IT RESOLVED that the incoming executive be instructed to enquire into the possibility of securing the funds necessary to engage a permanent secretary for the Association and that, if the money can be obtained, a

[1]See Chapter 9.

secretary be sought and appointed by the executive committee.

The executive was also instructed to establish a policy committee to plan a policy for the Association over a period of years.

It is also of significance that the Association accepted a report of a committee of the CNEA evaluating Canadian Legion War Services educational services courses. The committee, consisting of H. R. Low, Superintendent of Education for Manitoba, Professor A. B. Currie of McGill, and Dr. W. P. Percival, with the last the convenor, had been appointed by the CNEA President in November, 1940.

The post-convention meeting of the Board of Directors again indicated the increasing importance that the directorate was beginning to assume in CNEA affairs. Their number was now fourteen in addition to the usual officers. They met at 8.00 p.m. instead of 5.00 p.m., and their discussions occupy five pages instead of the page or so that formerly summarized their deliberations.

The Board received Dr. R. H. Coats, the Dominion Statistician, and Dr. J. E. Robbins of Dr. Coats' Education Division. These officials commended memoranda on statistics prepared by Dr. R. W. B. Jackson, Dr. J. E. Robbins, and Mr. H. W. Jamieson on a grant from the Canadian Council for Educational Research and indicated their intention of calling a conference of department of education officials to discuss more uniform bases of educational statistics.

It was significant, too, that Canadian Legion Educational Services (also Canadian Legion War Services educational services) sought permission from the directorate to extend its correspondence courses to personnel of the Merchant Navy, and that "the desired permission was gladly given."

The directors appointed a policy committee consisting of Dr. S. J. Willis, Dr. G. F. McNally, and Mr. A. R. Lord, and a budget committee. No reference is made in the minutes, however, to the resolution on obtaining funds to appoint a full-time secretary and to establish a secretariat.

It was at the following convention in Victoria in 1942 that Principal Cyril James of McGill, in his keynote address, asked the

CNEA, in his capacity as chairman of the Dominion Committee on Reconstruction, to appoint a committee to study the whole question of education in post-war reconstruction.

> In the light of the existing situation, and of the facts that I have touched upon, it is apparent that the Canada and Newfoundland Education Association must, if it is to play a significant part in the future educational development of this Dominion, turn its attention to some of the important problems that will arise after the war. I should like, as Chairman of the Committee on Reconstruction, to suggest that, at this convention, you set up a representative committee to make a comprehensive survey of education throughout the Dominion of Canada, and present its report directly to the Committee on Reconstruction. I should like to see all provinces and all types of educational activity (including universities and adult education) represented on that committee, and, if you decide to take action on my suggestion, I hope that the committee's terms of reference may be as wide as possible.

During the convention, the directors considered this request, along with a request by several national educational organizations that a central bureau of education be established by the CNEA. In consequence, the directors adopted two resolutions, as follows:

> That, as it is the duty and the privilege of the CNEA to meet the request of the Dominion Committee on Reconstruction for a Dominion-wide report on educational needs and for recommendations in respect thereof, the incoming Board of Directors be instructed to appoint immediately a committee to prepare and submit such a report.

> That the CNEA immediately establish a permanent secretariat of education at Ottawa; that the incoming directorate appoint a special committee for this purpose, subject to the approval of the executive committee of the directorate. The purpose of this secretariat shall be:
>
> (a) to be a medium of expression for the departments of education and the major national educational organizations in matters of common educational concern;
>
> (b) to confer with, co-operate with and advise the various committees and departments of the federal government on educational developments,

activities, and needs in times of both peace and war;

(c) to serve the departments of education and the national educational organizations as a central agency for the dissemination of information;

(d) to promote generally the cause of education throughout the country.

In expressing appreciation of his services to the retiring president, Dr. S. J. Willis, the new president, Dr. W. P. Percival, said in part: "The prospect of a permanent secretariat has come into being during your presidency, Dr. Willis—and that is a milestone indeed." While the hope of a secretariat was still further from being fulfilled than some of the directors may have thought, they none the less, following the convention, named a committee with authority to establish the permanent secretariat, subject to the approval of the executive committee.

It is doubtful if any single activity had a greater effect on the future development of the CNEA than the preparation and publication of the *Report of the Survey Committee Appointed to Ascertain the Chief Educational Needs of the Dominion of Canada*. Members of the committee were Dr. W. P. Percival, chairman, Dr. J. G. Althouse, secretary, Mr. B. O. Filteau, and Drs. Fletcher Peacock, G. F. Rogers, and G. F. McNally. The Canadian Teachers' Federation, Home and School, the Canadian Association for Adult Education, and the National Conference of Canadian Universities were invited to name representatives. The convention at Quebec in 1943 received and commended the report of this committee, which had first met on October 13, 1942, in Montreal, and again in Winnipeg on March 30, 1943. The committee's eighty-four-page report, having been made public after being approved by the directors and given to Dr. Cyril James that spring, was to serve in many ways as a blueprint for Canadian education following the end of the war. Some 10,000 copies of the Survey Report were printed.

The 1943 convention also heard an address by Mr. R. S. Lambert proposing the establishment of a national advisory council on school broadcasting in which Mr. Lambert asked the approval of the CNEA for the establishment of a national council of thirteen members; through an amendment a council of sixteen members was approved. The appointment of a committee to study the question of textbooks for Canadian history was proposed, and a third proposal was that the CNEA convention be brought to the attention of urban superintendents and inspectors for the purpose of encouraging them to attend, and thus increase their interest in the CNEA's work. The minutes of the meetings of the directors and of the executive in 1943–44 were printed as separate booklets, a new development. With respect to secretarial arrangements, the minutes of the directors' meeting following the Quebec convention report that Dr. McNally and Mr. Filteau were of the opinion that "it would be unwise to press for a secretariat." It was left to the executive to make whatever secretarial arrangements were possible and necessary. Then, making what would appear to be a flanking movement in this delicate matter, Dr. McNally said that the finances of the Association should be studied; Dr. Percival pointed out the growing interest of the provincial governments in the CNEA and suggested the possibility of obtaining increased grants from them; Dr. H. F. Munro thought efforts should be made to secure money for the new and larger activities of the CNEA. It was then moved by Dr. McNally and seconded by Dr. Munro:

1. That the president appoint a special committee on finance; (a) to study the problem of regular and equitable contributions from the provinces for the support of the work of the Association and to make recommendations based thereon, (b) to consider methods of securing adequate financial support for the work of the Canadian Council for Educational Research and to advise the executive as to action that should be taken.

2. That this committee be requested to begin work at once with a view to having action taken by the executive before legislative estimates are approved.

An executive committee was elected, with consideration being given to the distance members would have to travel. Elected were Dr. J. G. Althouse, Dr. C. C. Goldring, and Mr. B. O. Filteau. The executive by constitution consisted of seven members, four officers and three others.

The complete executive was present at meetings on October 29 and 30, 1943, at which time they constituted themselves as a special committee on finance. This committee recommended a budget of contributions proportionate to population based on the Ontario contribution of $2500 received in 1943. It was agreed that "requests should be made for gradually increasing amounts, not for markedly greater contributions." The budget was to be regarded as a plan or ideal to be placed before the deputy ministers, not as a set request. An item of $1200 was provided for a full-time stenographer, with the secretary-treasurer, who was part-time, to receive $600. This budget of $7710 was recommended to the Honorable Hubert Staines, Minister of Education for Saskatchewan, who had agreed to assist in raising funds.

The executive met not only through October 29 (Friday) but also on October 30. Concern was expressed that a large convention, to which many organizations sent representatives, might cause the Association to find itself overwhelmed. There was discussion of an educational policies committee, and it was decided that the executive be such a committee; their object would be to study trends and once or twice a year publish a statement that would serve to give educational leadership and to act as a unifying influence. Dr. Fletcher Peacock, probably without the benefit of a detailed study of the Association's inefficacy which would have staggered that enterprising man, said that the history of the CNEA showed "too little important work carried to an effective conclusion;" he hoped that the present meeting would mark a point of departure instituting a vigorous policy of leadership.

The executive met again on April 14 and 15. It was reported that a request for $5000 a year for two years had been made to the Carnegie Corporation to enable the CNEA to expand its facilities, although a footnote to the minutes says this was refused on May 19, 1944. It was decided to publish 5000 copies of a 32-page pamphlet on *Trends in Education During 1944*.

The twenty-second convention of the CNEA met in Toronto, October 11–13, 1944. It was a large convention with 236 members, 9 associate members, and 1 visitor in attendance. For the first time, the president, Dr. V. K. Greer, addressed himself to reviewing the substantial activities of the CNEA over the year. He attributed the growth of the Association to the decision, taken in 1941, to hold annual conventions, and to the issuance of the report of the survey committee.

In his review of CNEA activities in 1943–44, the president mentioned (1) the committee for the study of Canadian history textbooks which had held two meetings in Montreal, under Abbé Arthur Maheux; (2) a report on larger units of school administration; (3) efforts by the secretary to promote, through provincial departments of labor and education, advanced legislation to guard the employment of youth; (4) success in obtaining concessions in parcel post rates on visual aids; (5) concessions to educational publishers for priorities in obtaining materials for production; (6) priorities for departments and boards of education for purchasing radio receiving sets and for acquiring equipment used by the services after the war; (7) steps taken to assure that the CNEA should be consulted concerning a proposed United Nations organization for educational and cultural reconstruction; (8) the printing of the minutes of meetings of the executive and directors in the past year; (9) the establishment of the Canada-United States Committee on Education; (10) the efforts of a CNEA committee to facilitate arrangements for pension credit for teachers for service in more than one province.

Dr. Greer said:

> No other body is equipped to perform the functions of interchange, distribution, and co-ordination better than the CNEA. No other body enjoys the confidence of all departments of education and other provincial and national bodies to the extent that the CNEA does. No other body is as free from federal control as the CNEA.

At this important convention, Dr. Fletcher Peacock, Director of Education for New Brunswick, was elected president. Dr. Peacock announced that with the approval of his own minister and of the Board of Managing Directors of the Association, he would like to make two appeals to all departments of education:

> 1. That they utilize to the full the services which the CNEA can provide to co-ordinate effort and to strengthen the influence of education with the public

and with all civic and governmental authorities throughout the country;

2. That they give the Association adequate financial support.

During the following year, the policy of printing the directors' and executive's minutes was continued. The minutes show that a budget was approved and that an amount of $1000 was included for travelling expenses for the president. It was desired that the president be able to visit all provincial departments of education to secure the greater financial support needed by the Association. A statement by a sub-committee of the special committee on finance (Mr. Filteau, Dr. Greer, and the secretary-treasurer) on the aims of the Association and the duties of the secretary-treasurer was approved unanimously on the basis that it made explicit what had always been tacitly assumed. In the statement, emphasis was given to the CNEA's function in gathering and disseminating information, the encouragement of research, and the promotion of co-operation. Special mention was made of the constitutional rights of each province in education, and it was stated that "the policy of the Association has been and will continue to be such as to protect such constitutional rights."

At the executive meeting on November 20, 1944, a discussion held on a resolution regarding the setting-up of an international office of education established this field as an area of CNEA interest. In the interests of national unity, the executive at the same time agreed to promote "pen-pal" correspondence and the interchange of teachers.

The same meeting recorded approval for the early publication of a quarterly journal setting forth educational trends and important educational developments. It was also agreed that arrangements be made for a meeting of the ministers of education at the convention, if the attendance of at least five of these officials could be assured, and that steps be taken towards a comprehensive revision of the constitution at the next convention.

As an indication of continuing vigorous action in the CNEA at this time, the president said that he would place before Dr. M. E. LaZerte, of the Canadian Council for Educational Research, proposals for approaching life insurance companies for money for research on health and the Canadian Manufacturers' Association for money for research on vocational education. The president stated that in addition he intended to approach school boards of cities over 10,000 population for support for research and other activities and to invite their chief education officers to attend the 1945 convention. His visits to the western provinces had encouraged him to think that the proposed budget for 1945 would be acceptable to the provinces, and that there would be a 50 per cent increase in 1946.

At the executive meeting of March 12, 1945, the secretary-treasurer was asked, with reference to an international office of education, to write to the Prime Minister that, if education were to appear on the agenda of the United Nations at San Francisco, the CNEA would provide, or recommend, an adviser, if such were required. The CNEA was authorized to act for all provinces except Quebec in the allocation of war surplus material. It was decided that the constitution be revised by a committee under the chairmanship of Dr. J. G. Althouse.

The executive took note of the president's success in obtaining assurance of a budget that would permit the employment of a full-time secretary-treasurer, and recorded its congratulations. Dr. McNally was of the opinion that a full-time secretary should be appointed as from the date of the next convention, and he suggested that efforts be made to secure the services of Dr. C. E. Phillips.

The executive met again on April 9 and 10, 1945, in Toronto, in high hopes of continuing progress, but a grave problem presented itself. Even while the executive was meeting, a letter arrived from Mr. Filteau, the Quebec Deputy Minister, expressing regret that Quebec would be unable to give financial support to the Association as now envisaged; at the same time, Mr. Filteau tendered his resignation as vice-president and as a member of the executive.

This was indeed disheartening news. Nearly fifty-four years had passed since the organization of the CEA, and for twenty years before that there had been active consideration of the establishment of such an organization. In the early days of the DEA there had been repeated attempts to establish a federal bureau of education, and these efforts had only revealed each time what little hope there was of success.[1] The National Council of Education[2] had also attempted to bring about the establishment of a central office, but without success.

These efforts having been defeated long since, the time had at last arrived when the Association might itself hope to have a secretariat financed co-operatively by the provinces. The reaction of Quebec at this stage was a severe blow.

Whether, in the opinion of various provincial officials, concrete action on the appointment of a full-time secretary for the CNEA could no longer be postponed, or whether the members of the executive at that date were more determined and energetic than at any time in the past, or probably as a result of a combination of the two factors, the executive decided to proceed with their plans without the support of Quebec, much as they desired to have it. Tightening their belts, so to speak, because of the reduced funds that were now anticipated, the executive made financial adjustments in the budget, but they none the less agreed that a full-time secretary-treasurer should be sought.

At the same time it was decided that the president should call upon Mr. Filteau and try to persuade him to continue as a director of the Association.

[1]See Chapter 7.
[2]See Chapter 8.

Chapter 6

THE CEA ESTABLISHES A SECRETARIAT,
1945 - 1948

When the executive met again, on June 18, 1945, they found their situation much improved and, one might say, their courage and faith rewarded. Mr. Filteau found himself able to attend the meeting as a bearer of good news, stating that "the government of the province of Quebec would contribute to the financial support of the Association on the same basis as the other provinces."

The executive agreed to recommend to the directors the appointment of Dr. C. E. Phillips as the full-time secretary-treasurer at a salary of $6000 a year, his duties to begin on September 1, 1945. Dr. Phillips had been serving as the first part-time secretary, in contrast with his predecessors, who had been honorary.

The president announced that the Canadian Life Insurance Officers' Association would pay a grant of $10,000 for an extensive program of research on school health, and it was agreed to recommend Dr. A. J. Phillips, a lecturer at the Ontario College of Education, as director of the study at $4000, beginning on September 1, 1945. The CNEA secretary-treasurer would "administer the funds and arrange for office facilities and services."

At this important meeting, too, it was agreed to print a CNEA magazine, *Canadian Education*, in 2000 copies.

In the busy year of 1945, the executive met again on August 14. It was reported that all directors had approved by mail the appointment of Dr. C. E. Phillips, and policies were established for the administration of the CNEA office. It was now decided to publish 4000 copies of the first issue of *Canadian Education*. In view of the difficulties of transportation and accommodation attendant upon the conclusion of the war, the 1945 convention was cancelled, and arrangements were made instead for a meeting of the directors.

The directors met on November 19 and 20, 1945. Because there was no convention, the president, Dr. Fletcher Peacock, continued in office for a second year, and he presided at the meeting with twelve directors present. A number[1] of members of the Canadian Council for Educational Research were also present for joint meetings with the directors.

Approval was given to the setting-up, with the Canadian Public Health Association, of the National Committee for School Health Research, which, it is interesting to note, had had a Research Director since September 1. There was considerable discussion on research, which

> . . . touched on various aspects of research but focussed in due course on a motion of Dr. Goldring, seconded by Dr. Crutchfield, that the meeting go on record as approving the principle of accepting money for educational research from either governmental bodies or private sources, providing that the gifts and the conditions of the gifts are acceptable to the directors of the CNEA. Mr. Filteau expressed his opinion that the acceptance of funds for any educational purpose directly from the federal government rather than indirectly through the provincial government, would not be approved by his province.

The Canadian Council for Educational Research was disbanded and the CNEA Research Council created in its place, its powers to be defined by the CNEA and its funds reverting to that organization.[2]

There was discussion of the establishment of the United Nations Educational, Scientific, and Cultural Organization, and, continuing the CNEA's early interest in that organization, the secretary was instructed to bring the following motion to the attention of the Prime Minister:

> That the Canada and Newfoundland Education Association is the only organization representing the departments of education of the provincial governments,

---

[1]The minutes are vague on this matter—three members are mentioned by name.
[2]See Chapter 9.

which are the legally constituted authorities over education in Canada, and that as such the Canada and Newfoundland Education Association is the proper body to be consulted on any educational matter affecting Canada as a whole.

It was agreed that the letter should indicate the context of the resolution by reference to the United Nations Educational, Scientific, and Cultural Organization and that copies of the letter should be sent to ministers and deputy ministers of education in the various provinces.

It was reported at this time that the Board of Education of the city of Toronto was providing the CNEA with a school classroom[1] rent free, which would serve as an office for the Association.

At a meeting of the executive held on January 19 and 20, 1946, the president was able to report on his discussions with the Canadian Manufacturers' Association concerning a possible program of research on the relation of secondary schools to industry, and he read an outline that he had prepared for a study of this kind.

Dr. Althouse referred to the revision of the constitution that he was drafting for consideration of the next convention, his object being to ensure that "the vote at the convention would reflect the wishes of the provincial departments of education and would also be representative of all organized education throughout the Dominion as a whole."

Still another meeting of the executive was held, this time on March 13 and 14, 1946, in Toronto. Considerable discussion was devoted to a proposed revision of Article III of the constitution which "would restrict voting membership in order to safeguard control of the Association by the provincial departments of education." At the same time, the secretary-treasurer was instructed to define his duties in Section 5 in the light of his experience during the past year.

When the CNEA directors met in Edmonton on August 19, 1946, immediately before the convention, the new constitution of the Association was considered and approved, article by article and clause by clause.

[1]The Ryerson Public School.

At the convention itself, one of the most important features was the adoption of the new constitution. This revision was made as a result of the expanded activities of the Association, the appointment of a permanent secretary, and the provision by the provinces of a budget sufficient for this and related purposes. It constituted the CEA in such a way that its ultimate control lay with the departments of education.

Provision was made, however, for acceptance as *individual members* by the Association of almost anyone interested in education who was a member of an association or group of teachers, a school trustee, home and school member, adult educationist, university staff member, or a member of a national or provincial education association.

While this provision greatly enlarged the membership, control of the CEA, under this constitution, was placed in the hands of the departments of education, which were financing the Association, through the introduction of the term *representative delegate*. These delegates, who were also *individual members,* were the only ones with the right to vote on resolutions, elect officers, and amend the constitution. The term *representative delegate* not only prevented any particular group, such as teachers or trustees, or any large number of members in a convention city or province, from temporarily controlling the CEA; but it also gave recognition to organizations and groups whose interest and co-operation were being sought.

With the 1946 revision, the secretary-treasurer, later the executive secretary, as the full-time paid employee of the Association, ceased to be an elected director, in the same sense that the president and vice-president were elected, but became an appointee of the Board of Directors.

From the first, it had been agreed that the constitution of the CEA should be in both English and French, and it has always been printed by the Association in both languages. The constitution, as revised in 1946, is shown in Appendix A.

In introducing this revised constitution, Dr. Althouse explained that, with the generous consent of Newfoundland educators, the word "Newfoundland" was being dropped from the name of the

Association, although the constitution itself made it clear that there was no thought of dropping Newfoundland from the Association. Dr. Althouse went on to say:

> Now the rest of the constitution, as mentioned here, really seeks three rather simple aims. In the first place, the growth of interest in this organization over the past ten or twelve years has been remarkable. The primary purpose of this organization has always been to afford an opportunity for the administrators in this Dominion to have an agency for co-operation among the provincial departments of education, or rather among the officials of the different departments of education. Other persons have also joined in the deliberations of the Association, and, therefore, it has been thought that in the new constitution which is before us for consideration there should be two types of membership and only one kind will have voting rights. These voting members are called representative delegates, for they actually do represent groups of educators with kindred interests. The majority vote does rest with those groups which are customarily associated with education authorities, both provincial and local.
>
> At the same time the committee was faced with the very urgent necessity of not only retaining the policy of interesting others in the work of the organization, but the necessity of extending the field of those who might be interested in what the organization is trying to do. That objective, it is hoped, will be obtained in part through the individual memberships.
>
> There is another way in which the benefits of this organization might be extended, and that would be by way of a rather closer type of co-operation with other organizations whose objectives are similar to our own. Consequently, in Article IV which deals with the officers of the Association, you will find that the latch is off the door and that the Association makes a definite bid for active co-operation on the part of six very important and well-known organizations. Article IV includes an invitation to the six organizations to send representatives to our directorate who will have the full powers of other directors.

The constitution, thoroughly discussed over the preceding months by the executive and directors, was unanimously adopted.

A second feature of this first post-war convention was the presidential address by Dr. Fletcher Peacock, typically (for him) entitled *The CEA Looks Forward*. The address outlined the progress of the Association during the previous two years and set forth Dr. Peacock's views and hopes for its future.

At the directors' meetings following the convention, the Honorable C. H. Blakeny, Minister of Education for New Brunswick, spoke on behalf of the four ministers attending the convention. In their opinion, the CEA should give special attention to the provision of an information service in education, the inauguration of further research programs, and the promotion of a teacher-exchange scheme.

The secretary was authorized to request all deputy ministers to arrange for monthly news letters to be sent to the CEA to keep it abreast of educational developments, and to arrange for the regular mailing to the secretary of all documents, education acts, etc., likely to be of use.

During the fall and spring of 1946–47, the work of the CEA continued to progress rapidly. Indeed the services that the office was asked to undertake exceeded the resources of the Association's small staff. During the fall, the CEA agreed to take responsibility for the overseas exchange of teachers for all provinces except Ontario, which had been arranging such exchanges for some time. A discouraging development, however, was the announcement by Dr. C. E. Phillips that he proposed to resign as of June 30, 1947, his stated reason being the expiry of his leave of absence from the Ontario College of Education. Since Dr. Phillips, together with Dr. Fletcher Peacock, had played a major role in the establishment and early operation of the CEA's permanent office, the directors accepted Dr. Phillips' resignation with appreciable concern.

That the CEA office was already giving promise of expansion was indicated by the report in the spring of 1947 that nineteen school boards in sixteen cities had agreed to contribute an annual amount of $3000 to a CEA Information Service. When the executive met in the spring of 1947, there was considerable discussion of the increase in CEA work in relation to the number of staff and the amount of funds available.

By the time the CEA directors met on September 10, 1947, immediately before the convention in Quebec, the Association had a new executive secretary, Mr. F. K. Stewart, whose appointment, after an open competition, had been approved by the directors by mail. Mr. Stewart and Dr. Phillips served jointly in the CEA office for the month of June, Dr. Phillips' resignation becoming effective on June 30.

An important item of business at this meeting was a resolution, on Mr. Filteau's urging, that the directors viewed with favor the inclusion on the CEA staff of a bilingual officer of French-Canadian origin. This resolution, combined with concern over the high cost of printing a magazine and the time and staff required for editing it and other bulletins, led to the appointment of a budget committee to report to the directors' meeting immediately following the convention.

The twenty-fourth convention, a large one with a registration of 368, was held on September 11, 12, and 13, 1947. Because of the reluctance of the National Conference of Canadian Universities to ally itself with the CEA through representation on the CEA directorate, the constitution was amended at this meeting to delete provision for such a representative.

A resolution provided that the Board of Directors "consider the possibility of creating subdivisions of this organization to meet the needs of special groups within the framework of the CEA." The resolution provoked some discussion and was approved for study by the directors. The problem inherent in this resolution is one that has plagued the CEA over many years, and no satisfactory solution to it has yet been found.[1]

One of the most important matters discussed at the post-convention directors' meeting was the report of the budget committee previously mentioned. This committee recommended that a total of $21,000 be sought from the provinces, an increase of 40 per cent over the current budget. Mr. Filteau thereupon reminded the directors of their motion approving in principle the employment of a bilingual officer of French-Canadian origin. The budget committee explained that they did not feel that sufficient money for this purpose would

[1]See Chapter 10.

be forthcoming in provincial grants. After discussion, however, it was agreed that an amount of $25,000 should be sought from the provinces, an increase of 66⅔ per cent, so that the motion put forward by Mr. Filteau could be implemented.

The new secretary was requested to prepare a brief in support of a request to the provinces for this substantial increase in grants. With respect to this request, the secretary was able to report at the next directors' meeting, held in Winnipeg, September 27, 1948, that favorable replies had been received from all provinces except Quebec and Manitoba. Later in that year, both Quebec and Manitoba increased their grants to the Association.

Thus all the Canadian provinces, together with Newfoundland, co-operated in the principle of paying grants to the CEA in amounts proportionate to their populations, when a major increase was involved. Provincial grants for the year ending December 31, 1948, including the amounts from Quebec and Manitoba (not paid until early in 1949, but intended as 1948 contributions), totalled $25,963; Information Service grants from urban school boards amounted to $2,970.23, and subscriptions to *Canadian Education* and membership fees to $1,118.83. These sources of revenue provided an operating budget of $30,052.06.

Having regard to the amount of these receipts and to the responsible and reliable nature of their source, it may be considered that the CEA had achieved a reasonable degree of security as an organization, and hence was assured of the means of retaining a small staff and of carrying on a modest program of educational services to the provinces.

The further account of the development of the CEA as an organization since 1948 will be dealt with in Part III, as an aspect of the CEA's role in Canadian education. The events described to this point show the long, and at times none too vigorous, struggle of Canadian educationists to work together towards the solution of common problems as citizens of one country. A first step in developing methods of co-operation lay in the provision of a small continuing staff which, however inadequate in itself, might serve to provide a link with past efforts and to give encouragement to new ones.

PART II

Special Problems of Organization

Chapter 7

PROPOSALS FOR A FEDERAL BUREAU
OF EDUCATION

The CEA began as an association of teachers, though it never had much success in this capacity. It was not until its constitution was revised in 1918 that the organization had any stated aim at all, and then it was limited to the amiable but vague ideal of promoting better understanding. While efforts of the CEA to serve as a means of collating educational information began in 1934, it was not until 1946 that the constitution included as one of its aims, "To collect and make available to educators in Canada and Newfoundland information on educational developments in Canada and elsewhere."[1]

Yet Canadian educators met to establish their first national organization at a meeting in Toronto of the National Education Association of the United States. They were acquainted with a number of American educators, an acquaintanceship that has since vastly expanded and deepened. They were familiar with school and other educational texts produced in the United States, and many Canadians, particularly those who were government employees, had high regard for and made much use of the publications of the Bureau of Education in Washington.

It might be expected, therefore, that at early meetings of the CEA, attention would be given to the matter of a central office of education for Canada. Thus at the convention in Halifax in 1898, J. M. Harper, LL.D., Government Inspector of High Schools for Quebec, addressed the delegates on the subject of *A National or Central Bureau of Education for Canada.* "The organization of a

[1]See Appendix A.

national or central bureau of education," said Dr. Harper, not
without optimism, "has become at last a practical question." Pointing out that the British North America Act, presumably in assign-
ing education exclusively to the provinces, was in part a compromise
and not necessarily a solution, he argued that provincialism was
too strong a factor in Canadian life after thirty years of Confederation. Even apart from this, Dr. Harper thought a central office could
be established without infringing upon the constitution. He outlined with high praise the activities of the United States Bureau
and emphasized that it had no constitutional oversight of the state
school systems. A Canadian Educational Bureau would concern
itself primarily with collecting statistics and with showing the
progress of education in comparative form in the different provinces.

Dr. Harper urged that a committee be formed to take charge
of the matter and press it upon the federal authorities. Subsequently a committee was appointed to consider and report on the
establishment of a central bureau, the committee consisting of
G. U. Hay (New Brunswick), T. Kirkland (Ontario), D. Mac-
Intyre (Manitoba), J. B. Calkin (Nova Scotia), Dr. J. M. Harper
(Quebec), and the Honorable G. W. Ross (Ontario).

This committee reported orally to the next convention in 1901,
but there is no record of the report other than in a second address
by Dr. J. M. Harper on the same subject. The committee was instructed to continue.

In an address at the next convention, Dr. Harper pointed out
that considerable publicity had been given to the idea of an educational bureau, but that he recognized the prejudice existing
against an office that might interfere with systems of education
under the sole control of the respective provinces. He reported
that a deputation of the Honorable G. W. Ross (Ontario), Dr.
McCabe (Principal of the Ottawa Normal School), and others
had waited upon Sir Wilfrid Laurier with a view to obtaining his
agreement to such an office. The Prime Minister had said he would
look into the matter.

Dr. Harper, in so vigorously promoting the cause of a central
federal bureau of education, expressed such high hopes of what
a bureau would accomplish that he undoubtedly alarmed some of

his more conservative colleagues. He spoke, for instance, of the importance of a "common national school" and accused his opponents of having a policy of suspicion, founded upon provincialism, which stood, not as a lion, but as a kind of dog-in-the-manger, in the way of educational advancement. "Canada," he said on this occasion in 1901, "is the only civilized nation, or quasi-nation, in the world which cannot tell in co-ordinated detail the story of its annual educational movements." Dr. Harper listed the functions of a bureau as (1) improving and co-ordinating the various school systems; (2) collecting all documents on educational developments and preparing historical memoranda; (3) preparing an annual report and collecting and preparing statistics; (4) making known new developments in other countries; (5) making known to the general public information on education—school laws, use of school funds, teacher qualifications, methods of instruction, school plans, and so forth; (6) publicizing trends in education relating to industry; (7) publishing addresses delivered at conventions and other gatherings.

The proposals put forward by Dr. Harper were formally opposed by the Honorable P. Boucher de la Bruère, Superintendent of Public Instruction for the province of Quebec. Dr. de la Bruère said that these suggestions for a central bureau in Ottawa had been urged since 1897, and he pointed out that those pressing for a bureau must be aware the majority of people in Quebec were antagonistic to such a proposal. The Superintendent then placed the attitude of Quebec on the CEA records:

> At its sitting in the month of May, 1899, that distinguished body (the Catholic Committee of the Council of Public Instruction) composed of all the bishops of the province and of prominent laymen, being called upon to state its views with regard to the advisability of this measure, unanimously adopted the following resolution on the motion of Honorable Mr. Justice Langelier seconded by Monseigneur Laflamme, a former rector of Laval University.
>
> "That this Committee, after taking communication at the Superintendent's request of the memorial which the executive committee of the Dominion Educational Association wish to present to the Prime Minister of Canada,

asking him to establish a bureau of education under the control of the federal government, are of opinion that the establishment of such a federal department is neither constitutional nor desirable."

There is no ambiguity in the above resolution and there can be no misconception with regard to the opinion so clearly expressed by the Committee of the Council of Public Instruction which, in our province, represents the great majority of the population.

Dr. de la Bruère objected to Dr. Harper's proposal in part because it showed a desire to imitate the United States Bureau; what might be suitable for the United States might not suit Canada at all; nor did any provision for such a bureau exist under the Canadian Constitution. If the collection of statistics were the sole aim, provision for their collection already existed under Canadian statutes. Dr. de la Bruère thought that something much more than this was being sought, and he quoted excerpts from Dr. Harper's addresses which had been printed in the daily press. He called the proposal to establish some central federal office "a violation of the spirit and letter of the Constitution of 1867 and an infringement of the autonomy of the provinces."

Should there be a Chief Commissioner of Education, Dr. de la Bruère said, the question might well arise as to who he would be. Because of certain excellences in education in Quebec, the commissioner might with some justice, the Superintendent pointed out, be a French-Canadian. Dr. de la Bruère doubted if such a person would be acceptable to some of the provinces, and thus implied that Quebec might not unnaturally be concerned if a commissioner of English origin were appointed. In brief, Dr. de la Bruère felt that no application should be made to the federal government for a central bureau when strong objections existed, "both from the standpoint of the particular interests of the provinces and from that of the Constitution by which we are governed."

No reference was made to a central bureau of education in the general sessions of the next convention in Winnipeg in 1904; neither was there present a representative of French-speaking Quebec. However, Dr. Harper was present and addressed the Inspection and Training Section of the DEA on the need for a

Dominion bureau, though the Proceedings state: "He (Dr. Harper) recognized that, at the present time, the establishment of such a bureau was impossible," and he suggested that, until its necessity was recognized by all the provinces, the DEA try to carry on the work of such an office. However reluctant and incapable for many years the DEA proved to be in carrying out this suggestion, Dr. Harper showed himself in these remarks to be something of a prophet.

At the convention in Toronto in 1907, no departmental officials from Quebec are shown as being present or even as members, although the membership list shows impressive representation from all other provinces. The Principal of Macdonald College, Dr. J. W. Robertson, was elected DEA vice-president, and one of his staff a director. Again at the 1909 convention there was no representation from French-speaking Quebec.

That proposals within the DEA to press for a federal bureau of education were closely related to the defection of Quebec French-speaking members from the Association is evident from some remarks made at the 1909 convention. This meeting gave greater and more intelligent attention to the best form of organization for the Association than did any other deliberation prior to 1942. Mr. A. E. Lang, Victoria University, Toronto, in referring to a central bureau of education in Ottawa, said that he would very much like to see one, but "I think the past history of our Association shows that to be impossible . . . Unfortunately we are divided, not only by distance but also by race and creed, and I think it would be unwise, to say the least, to re-open this question *when it has already caused considerable trouble in the DEA.*"[1]

Dr. W. A. McIntyre of Winnipeg thought that a federal bureau should be organized in Ottawa, to which there were, in his opinion, no valid objections. If this were not possible, Dr. McIntyre felt that the provinces ought to combine in supporting such a bureau. Dr. A. H. MacKay, Nova Scotia Superintendent, believed that there should be a federal bureau, though he said that he was not present when it was previously discussed; its principal function should be the collection of educational statistics. Mr. D. S. Mackenzie,

[1]Italics ours.

Alberta Deputy Minister, and Mr. D. P. McColl, Saskatchewan
Deputy Commissioner, supported the idea of a central bureau of
education operated either by the federal or, preferably, by the
provincial authorities.

As explained in Chapter 2, the DEA did not meet again until
1913. Once more the importance of a Dominion educational bureau
was stressed, this time in an address by Dr. A. H. MacKay who
said that a bureau "is now very desirable, if not indeed necessary."
Dr. MacKay thought there was no objection to a bureau as such,
but only to its possible interference with the provinces in educational matters. No discussion ensued on this subject at the time,
however.

When the DEA met again in 1917, it had in attendance official
representatives from each province. For the first time since 1901,
French-speaking Quebec was represented, the delegate being the
Honorable Cyrille Delâge, Superintendent of Education.

A principal feature of the convention was a round table conference on *The Organization of a Federal Bureau of Education.* Dr.
A. H. MacKay, Superintendent of Education for Nova Scotia,
introduced the discussion and repeated his arguments, presented on
previous occasions, on the need for a compilation of education laws
and statistics; he expressed his regret that Canadians had to rely
so heavily on publications of the United States Bureau. The
Dominion government, he pointed out, was now making some
small start on educational statistics; this was at least a beginning,
and the Dominion should be encouraged to do more.

Dr. MacKay was supported by Dr. J. F. White, who maintained
that every province had something to learn in education from the
others. "If we are going to be a country," he said, "we must have
some ideals in common. So long as we remain as at present, education is rather parochial, rather local, than even provincial or
nation-wide."

Pointing out, in addition to this, that Canada would need
to re-absorb many soldiers after the war, as well as deal with
an influx of immigrants, Dr. White thought that this representative
meeting should make suggestions to the government as to how a
central office could help in these matters.

Dr. H. L. Brittain delivered a major address on the subject of *A National Clearing House for Education*.[1] He deplored the reliance of Canadians on reports and experiments done in other countries and said that "the information most worthwhile for Canada, and most adapted to Canadian needs, must be developed by Canadians in Canada."

In commenting on proposals for a federal office, Mr. Delâge, on behalf of Quebec, said smoothly that this was the most interesting, if not the newest, question before the DEA. He reviewed previous proposals on this matter, pointing out that his predecessor in 1901 had firmly opposed a "bureau of education in Ottawa, under the direction of the federal government." The Catholic Committee in Quebec considered such an office unconstitutional, and neither necessary nor desirable. Mr. Delâge then quoted the pertinent resolution of the Committee passed in May, 1899, so that there would be "no ambiguity and no mistake as to the nature of his mandate."

Mr. Delâge's remarks were as firm as they were suave. In referring to the Constitution, he said, "Section 93 of the British North America Act, according exclusive rights to the provinces in matters of education, has not been amended, so far as I am aware." With reference to statistics, however, Mr. Delâge concurred in the opinion that the federal government had power to make arrangements with the provinces for their collection, and in this matter he was sure that his government would do all that was required.

After further discussion, it was agreed that it would be desirable for each province to learn something of the educational work in other provinces and that means should be found to accomplish this. The question was then referred to the resolutions committee which subsequently put forward the resolution that recognized the purposes of the DEA to be the promotion of common educational interests and of better understanding of the educational programs of the other provinces on the part of each province and recommended that in order to achieve these purposes, the DEA should be reorganized as a representative association.

In view of Quebec's strong opposition to a federal bureau of education and the extended absence of Quebec officials from the

[1]See page 29.

DEA meetings after proposals for such an office in 1901, it is interesting to note their apparent satisfaction with the CEA as reconstituted in 1918. Although a federal bureau of education was a principal topic of discussion in 1917, the convention in 1918 was attended by the Honorable Cyrille Delâge,[1] Quebec Superintendent of Education, and J. N. Miller, French secretary of the Committee of Public Instruction, as well as by the English secretary, Dr. G. W. Parmelee, and by the chairman of the Protestant Committee of Public Instruction. Some small progress was now reported on the collection of educational statistics by the federal government, and the CEA's approval was sought for the appointment of an educationist for that work.[2] It was apparent that CEA members, or more properly provincial officials meeting at the CEA convention, accepted the fact that a federal bureau modelled on the one at Washington was not then a possibility for Canada; accordingly they were prepared to accept and encourage an embryonic office for educational statistics as a useful compromise.

Provincial officials at subsequent CEA meetings occasionally made reference to a federal bureau of education, but this was done, as it were, in passing, and was wistful rather than purposeful or argumentative. For instance in 1927, the president, Dr. Robert Fletcher, spoke of the importance of research and of the need for more knowledge of teacher qualifications and types of school buildings. "Here," he said, "is where a Dominion bureau of education could render a fine service to all the provinces without trespassing upon any of our educational prerogatives."

Frequent reference was made to the autonomy of each province in education, and to the value of CEA meetings where information and ideas could be exchanged without coercion. In addressing the CEA in 1929, Mr. C. J. Magnan, Inspector-General of Catholic Normal Schools for Quebec, said that he observed with satisfaction that developments in the CEA since 1901 had been made within the purpose of its founders, namely, the promotion of the cause of education while respecting the autonomy of each province.

[1] Mr. Delâge is shown as a delegate on page 7 of the Proceedings, and is reported by Mr. Miller on page 127 as being sick in Quebec from overwork on a Victory Loan. Intent in this case must have been taken for the deed. Mr. Miller stated that Mr. Delâge "takes a very great interest in this Association" and, as a matter of fact, the records over the years show him as a regular participant in and frequent contributor to CEA affairs.
[2] See page 31.

This was a period (1920–1934) in the affairs of the CEA when there was increasing interest among its membership in each province in the educational programs and developments in other provinces. The door through which steps might be taken towards the establishment of a federal bureau through CEA encouragement remained closed. But pressure grew for some means to be found for the collection and distribution of information on educational progress in different provinces. While no substantial advance was being made towards this goal, the CEA convention was becoming more and more an occasion when educational information was exchanged. Departments reported briefly at each convention on educational developments and trends that had become apparent in the interval between meetings, and these reports were printed in the convention Proceedings. As time passed, the feeling grew deeper and more widespread that provincial boundaries ought not to be provincial barriers to the collation of information about Canadian education. For instance, Dr. A. M. Scott, Superintendent of Schools, Calgary, wrote in a letter to the CEA as early as October 27, 1922, that the provincial departments of education should establish a permanent central office which could co-operate with the statistical branch of the census office in Ottawa; this office "should be a clearing house for educational information and statistics for all Canada." Such feelings as these, however, were as yet far from strong enough to bring about the establishment of any office in education, even of an interprovincial nature.

In this same period there waxed and waned an organization known as the National Council of Education,[1] in which many senior educational officials participated. There was hope for a time that the National Council itself might establish a clearing house in education, and the Council, too, explored the idea of a federal bureau. In this connection, it is interesting to note a statement by Mr. Vincent Massey, its immediate past president, to the National Council in 1926. "For nine years the Council has been urged to secure the establishment of a Canadian Bureau of Education. Due, however, either to a misunderstanding of some of the functions of such a bureau, or the failure to appreciate the

[1]See Chapter 8.

importance of others, the idea has not met with sufficient support to secure its adoption. For this reason I recommend that the project be abandoned."

Two developments, in addition to the departmental reports mentioned above, served to remove, after 1934, the agitation for a federal bureau that had on many occasions occupied the CEA's attention. One was the greater activity of the Education Branch of the Dominion Bureau of Statistics. Dr. John E. Robbins from that office attended the 1936 convention, inviting the CEA members to suggest in what ways the Education Branch could be of greater usefulness, and forecasting a national meeting on educational statistics which subsequently took place. The other was the development of proposals, beginning in 1936, to establish a broadly-based Dominion Bureau of Educational Research.[1]

Both these developments held considerable promise. The Education Branch very gradually provided increasing service, and the Bureau of Research (The Canadian Council for Educational Research) flourished briefly through the early part of World War II before being supplanted in large part by other CEA activities.

The question of a federal bureau of education did not arise again in the CEA until the convention in Victoria in 1942, coinciding with the CEA's momentous decision to undertake a survey of Canada's educational needs. A convention conference group of school superintendents and inspectors put forward a resolution that the Board of Directors approach the Dominion government with regard to the establishment of a bureau of education. After considering this proposal, the directors reported that they had resolved to establish immediately a permanent secretariat of education at Ottawa. While the directors agreed that this might not satisfy the desire of the Canadian Teachers' Federation for a bureau of education, nor, indeed, the wishes of some other groups for such a bureau, there were conflicting opinions as to what form such a bureau should take.

A much more detailed report on this meeting is available in CEA office files than in the CNEA Proceedings. The former reveal that several deputations submitted requests to the CNEA directors

[1]See Chapter 9.

at an evening meeting on September 14, 1942, asking the CNEA to take steps to establish a central bureau of education. These deputations were from the Canadian Teachers' Federation, the National Conference of Canadian Universities, the Canadian Federation of Home and School, and the Canadian Council of Education for Citizenship. Since the spokesman for the last-named organization, Dr. E. A. Corbett, was also the secretary of the Canadian Association for Adult Education, the report in the CEA files assumes that he spoke for that body as well.

Before these deputations (with the exception of the Canadian Teachers' Federation) put forward their views, Principal Cyril James of McGill, chairman of the Dominion Committee on Post-War Reconstruction, invited the CNEA to establish a Survey Committee. The committee was established, and shortly produced the significant Survey Report.

After the request for the establishment of a Survey Committee had been received, vice-president W. E. McNeill, speaking for the National Conference of Canadian Universities, said that the universities would like to see a central bureau of education established. The other organizations put forward similar views.

The Honorable C. H. Blakeny, Minister of Education for New Brunswick, representing the Canadian Council of Education for Citizenship, said that he was anxious to see a central bureau established at once "to safeguard provincial rights in education." At the directors' meetings there was general agreement that there should be a central office, but there were "sharply opposed opinions" as to whether the office should be financed entirely by the provinces, primarily by the provinces with some federal aid, or primarily or entirely by the federal government.

A special committee was appointed, consisting of Mr. A. R. Lord, Mr. B. O. Filteau, the Honorable C. H. Blakeny, and Dr. G. F. McNally, whose task it was to resolve the differences revealed in the discussions and also to prepare a resolution with respect to the educational survey requested by Principal James.

Regarding the central bureau, the committee recommended:

> That the CNEA immediately establish a permanent secretariat of education at Ottawa; that the incoming

directorate appoint a special committee for this purpose, subject to the approval of the executive committee of the directorate. The purpose of this secretariat shall be:

(a) to be a medium of expression for the departments of education and the major national education organizations in matters of common educational concern;

(b) to confer with, co-operate with, and advise the various committees and departments of the federal government on educational developments, activities, and needs in times of both peace and war;

(c) to serve the departments of education and the national educational organizations as a central agency for the dissemination of information;

(d) to promote generally the cause of education throughout the country.

This recommendation was approved by the directors and by the convention as a whole.

Thus in 1942, for the first time since 1917, a proposal to try to promote the establishment of a federal bureau was strongly advanced at a CEA meeting, this time by a number of very influential bodies. It was indicative of the change in the management of CEA affairs that the proposal was rejected on this occasion at a meeting of CNEA directors, rather than in open convention. In recognition, however, of the wide-spread feeling that a federal office of education was a practical necessity, the CNEA at least made a declaration of intent to establish instead its own liaison office.

By 1944, the CNEA had embarked upon a wide range of activities. It was reported that in the past year the secretary-treasurer had devoted half his time to the work of the Association, travelling 6000 miles and writing some 1500 individual letters; he had employed, at Association expense, a full-time stenographer.

The president, Dr. V. K. Greer, referred to "the ever-widening service rendered by CNEA," and stated that "other bodies and individuals are constantly calling for a co-ordinating agency which will provide an interchange of information across the Dominion and Newfoundland."

It is clear that the members of the CNEA, in so far as they expressed opinions on this matter, looked increasingly on the organization itself as the focal point for interprovincial educational activity. To some, who had no apprehensions about a federal bureau, the efforts of the CNEA may have seemed a poor substitute for a larger federal office with the weight of the federal government behind it; to others, the CNEA may have seemed to serve as a means of intercommunication until the Association developed greater resources, or until a federal office eventually made its appearance; and to still others, the CNEA, an extremely modest unofficial agency completely controlled by the departments of education and delicately sensitive to their views and wishes, may have seemed to offer a not too inconvenient compromise in answer to recurrent demands for a bureau of education controlled by the federal government.

Because of post-war developments in the CEA, combined with the growth in certain limited directions of the Education Division of the Dominion Bureau of Statistics, no further proposals with respect to a federal bureau of education have been made within the Association itself.

This account of proposals for a federal bureau of education is naturally limited to the CEA's interest in and attitude toward such an office. No attempt is made to examine the arguments for or against a federal office. In addition, it is not known whether the federal government would at any time have been receptive to proposals for the establishment of such an office. It can be said, however, that the views put forward several times within the CEA, certainly in the case of Quebec, were official or at least semi-official. It is also clear from the records that federal officials were reluctant to move in educational matters, even concerning educational statistics, without encouragement and indeed endorsation either from the CEA as an organization or from senior educational officials in conference at the CEA.

Chapter 8

THE NATIONAL COUNCIL OF
EDUCATION

During the 1920's, an organization known as the National Council of Education (sometimes "*on* Education") rose in the educational skies, relatively speaking, like a fireworks rocket, made a brief brilliant display, and then faded away. It vastly outshone the Canadian Education Association, a sombre and unobtrusive enough organization even in the best of times—and in the twenties the CEA was far from its best.

In the spring of 1917, at a dinner given by the Lieutenant-Governor of Manitoba, Sir James Aikins, a movement was begun for the holding of a conference on the relationship of Canadian education to character and citizenship. A committee was formed to make preparations for such a conference.

> It was not anticipated that the proposed conference itself would provide a definite solution to the difficult problems involved, but it was hoped that . . . adequate sanction might be secured from such a gathering for the creation of a permanent body which would address itself in a continuous way to the study and illumination of the problem.[1]

Steps were taken to arouse public interest in the proposed organization, and groups of citizens favorable to such a conference were organized in some forty towns and cities in the various provinces. A sum of approximately $10,000 was obtained by individual subscriptions, and Rotary Clubs agreed to provide further financial assistance; this amounted to $27,570. The conference cost

---

[1]Report of the Proceedings of the National Conference on Character Education in Relation to Citizenship.

a substantial figure, including $5534 for advertising and $4070 for expenses of speakers.

The first meeting, held in Winnipeg, October 20–22, 1919, was called "A National Conference on Character Education in Relation to Citizenship," and was under the patronage of His Grace the Duke of Devonshire, Governor-General of Canada. "The conference was a concerted effort to rally the best public opinion behind the schools of the Dominion, it being apparent that the education departments could not be fully effective unless supported by a continuous public enthusiasm on behalf of education. To generate that enthusiasm, it appeared essential to define and articulate something of a national conception of the goal or objective of Canadian education."

The purpose of the conference was described as follows:

> The ideal to be achieved is the ideal of Canadian citizenship which will make of life for all a fellowship, and not the destructive, dehumanizing competition which characterizes the present day . . . The conference of 1919 contended that there is immediate need of a regeneration of spiritual ideals in social life, a recognition of the intrinsic value of personality. In this much-needed regeneration, the whole-hearted co-operation of all educational authorities is essential . . . Education itself must be endowed with a high moral purpose.

The conference was attended by "upwards of 1500 accredited delegates of public bodies of all kinds" from all parts of Canada. The audience (delegates and general public) at no session fell below 2000, and at one evening session rose to 5000. The gathering was reported to be of a widely diversified representative character.

Among the speakers were Sir Robert Falconer, President of the University of Toronto, Dr. G. W. Parmelee, Archbishop Samuel Pritchard Matheson, the Honorable Cyrille Delâge, university professors, normal school principals, school superintendents, soldiers, and others. The meeting received greetings from the National Education Association and from the Commissioner of Education of the United States.

As a result of this conference there was created a National Council (of Education) of fifty members, thirty-six of whom were

elected from the provinces by the conference and fourteen by the
Council itself. Members of the Council included various persons
long active in the DEA, such as Dr. Parmelee, the Honorable
Cyrille Delâge, Dr. J. A. Snell, and Inspector F. Peacock of New
Brunswick.

After active discussions stretching over several sessions, the
conference passed the following resolution:

> That for purposes of educational investigation and as
> a clearing-house for educational data, a national bureau
> be established under the direction of the National
> Council of the conference, and that such a bureau
> be maintained by voluntary support and such financial
> assistance as may be given by provincial and Dominion
> governments without any restrictions as to policy.

In furtherance of this resolution, a meeting of the deputy
ministers of education was held in Quebec by invitation of that
province in November, 1920, and a meeting of ministers and
deputy ministers of education was later held in Toronto (October
30, 31, and November 1, 1922) by invitation of the government of
Ontario. At the former meeting, it was proposed that the bureau
be administered by a departmental committee of the deputy
ministers of education of the various provinces, while the latter
meeting resulted in the following resolution:

> That this conference grant the request of the National
> Council of Education to respectfully submit to the govern-
> ments of the provinces the question whether they are in
> favor of the establishment of a bureau of education for
> all or any of the purposes outlined below:
>
> 1. (a) The collection and publication of reports on
>   educational matters, problems and develop-
>   ment in the provinces of the Dominion,
>   throughout the British Empire, and in other
>   parts of the world.
>   (b) Such other functions as may be delegated to it
>   from time to time by common consent of all
>   the provincial departments of education, and
> 2. That the provincial governments favoring the
>   establishment of such a bureau appoint a delegate
>   to a further conference to consider and report to
>   their respective governments upon plans for the
>   organization and maintenance of such a bureau if

found practical, and that the necessary correspondence to carry these proposals into effect be
conducted by Major F. J. Ney, secretary of the
present conference.

From this point on, the status and activities of the Council
become somewhat difficult to follow, though, having regard to the
above resolution, this should not be surprising to perceptive readers.
A bulletin reporting on progress says ". . . the great question to be
decided was how to organize a bureau which would be acceptable
in its constitution to the nine departments . . . Progress towards a
solution has undoubtedly been made, but the solution proposed
has yet to meet with the approval of the provinces . . ." At the 1920
meeting of deputy ministers, it was planned to have both a French
and an English department, each with its own secretary. The Ontario
government voted a grant to provide an English secretary, who was
appointed, and Manitoba made office space available and assisted
with the purchase of equipment. These offices appear to have been
used for a time in the early 1920's, and reference is made in a
National Council of Education bulletin to the accumulation of a
reference library of considerable size.

However, at the second conference, held in Toronto in 1923, it
was voted that:

This conference reaffirms the resolution passed at the
Winnipeg Conference in 1919 in relation to the formation
of an educational bureau under interprovincial control
and instructs the incoming executive to continue its
negotiations for the purpose of bringing such a bureau
into existence.

In a prologue to the conference, Mr. Vincent Massey, the
president, is reported as saying:

There is much to be gained from the diversity of a
system in which nine provinces independently work out
their own problems and exchange their ideas. But there
must be some means by which these provinces can exchange their ideas—some clearing-house of information
for this purpose, and also an agency through which to tell
the outside world what is going on in Canadian education
and to borrow appropriate ideas from outside.

In another address to the conference, the retiring president, Dr.
W. J. Bulman, after describing the proposed bureau as "an inter-

provincial bureau through the co-operation of the various departments of education," goes on:

> The composition of a bureau so constituted would be
> a guarantee of educational knowledge, experience, and
> wisdom in the administration of its activities. The ac-
> cumulated experience and information of each province
> would be available for all. The bureau would have official
> sanction and recognition. At the same time there would
> be no suspicion of Dominion intervention in education,
> a point on which all the provinces are acutely sensitive.
> The expense would be borne by the several provinces so
> that it would fall heavily on none. In this way, it would
> be possible to establish an agency which . . . would be
> organized and equipped to study current educational
> movements and tendencies, the results of such study to be
> available in the form of special reports for the information
> of local education authorities and teachers and citizens in-
> terested in the betterment of schools . . . The work of the
> bureau would be done by competent judges and reliable
> witnesses and would be free from all suspicion of bias . . .

The report of this meeting was published by the Oxford University Press, under the title *Education and Life*. The speakers included Mr. Vincent Massey, Sir Michael Sadler, *Tradition and
Freedom,* Sir Henry Newbolt, *Literature and Humanity,* Dr. H. M.
Tory, *The Valuation of Education,* Dr. H. J. Cody, *The Intrinsic
Value of Personality,* Sir Robert Baden-Powell, *Goodwill Training
for Citizenship,* and Lord Robert Cecil, *The League of Nations.*
The conference was a massive affair, and apparently Massey Hall
was crowded for a number of the addresses. Financing appears to
have been provided by the Toronto Rotary Club.

In view of later developments in the CEA, it is interesting to
note that one of the objects of this conference is described as:

> To pave the way for annual public conferences of a
> more professional character at which detailed discussion
> can be entered into on the great educational problems of
> the day, and on the development of education in other
> parts of the world.

The third conference of the National Council was held in
Montreal, April 5–10, 1926, under the patronage of the Governor-
General, with the Honorable Vincent Massey as president,

and Mr. E. W. Beatty as chairman. Addresses on a variety of topics were given by distinguished speakers from abroad, including the Duchess of Atholl, Parliamentary Under-Secretary of the Board of Education, Dr. Etienne Gilson from the Sorbonne, Sir Hugh Percy Allen from Oxford University, as well as by leading Canadian educationists.

Some business sessions were held, in addition to the public addresses given, but the great enthusiasm for a central bureau of education had been thoroughly dampened. It was reported that the Council had decided "to abandon the establishment of a central bureau of education. The conference held that it would be improper for the Council to interfere in any way with the exclusive jurisdiction in education guaranteed by the British North America Act to provincial governments." It was believed that it would be preferable for the Council to concern itself with the promotion of good citizenship.

It was agreed that the next triennial conference should be held in Halifax, but it was held instead in Victoria and Vancouver in April, 1929. The theme of the fourth conference was "Education and Leisure," and addresses and discussions were devoted chiefly to recreation as a means towards education. As at previous conferences, there were present a number of distinguished visitors, this time from the United Kingdom, Australia, New Zealand, India, and several foreign countries. No record is available of any business discussions.

The indications are, however, that the Council, which in 1926 had given up the idea of a central office in education, had now begun to dissipate its energy, never too specifically directed anyway, in a number of different and vague activities. No further conferences were held. Undoubtedly, even if other causes were not sufficient, the economic depression of the thirties would have had a strongly inhibiting effect on the kind of spectacular conference that the National Council promoted.

The Toronto Reference Library contains only three publications of the National Council dated later than 1929. Two of these are pamphlets, one on the foreign film in Canada and the other on foreign magazines in Canada; both of these arise from resolutions made at the 1929 conference, and are dated 1931. The third publication is a depressing little illustrated booklet of thirteen pages entitled *Salute to Britain* and published on the occasion of St. George's Day, April 20, 1941. Although carrying the name of the Council, the booklet contains no information about the organization itself.

The National Council had taken as a major purpose one of the early purposes of the CEA, the establishment of a central office in education, supported by the Council, or the provinces, or the federal government. It had behind it not only the support of outstanding educationists, but also of leading figures in business and government. During the period of its ascendance, it unquestionably cast a shadow over the CEA. The CEA met in Ottawa in 1922 because a meeting of the National Council made it convenient for the CEA then and inconvenient on other occasions. CEA members had frank hopes that the Council would succeed in doing what they themselves had failed to do.

Originally financed by business men and service clubs, the National Council, after a short period, exhausted these funds; it thereupon appealed to the provincial governments for assistance, which was not forthcoming. For these reasons, the National Council provides an interesting case history of the efforts and subsequent failure of a vigorous and broadly-based organization to establish a central bureau of education.

In conclusion it may be said that the National Council, which enjoyed such mushroom growth in the twenties, has now vanished as an organization. The CEA secretary-treasurer, Dr. C. E. Phillips, in a report to the president about a trip to western Canada in 1946, stated that Major F. J. Ney was at that time visiting the departments of education for the purpose of re-establishing his National Council of Education. A grant of $1000 was being sought from Alberta for this purpose. Major Ney, according to this report, was promoting the Council as the exclusive agency to deal with the Dominion government on matters pertaining to UNESCO, and claimed to have had an enthusiastic reception from the ministers of education. The CEA secretary, not unreasonably, took the view that the Council was in no way representative of Canadian education, although he paid tribute to Major Ney's work in overseas teacher exchange.

In 1947, Major Ney suggested in a letter to the CEA president that the National Council and the CEA should amalgamate under some such name as the Canadian Council of Education. The directors expressed appreciation of Major Ney's earlier work in promoting teacher exchange and Empire unity, but said they did not see how it would be possible for the CEA to be affiliated in some way with the Council. Since that time there appears to be no evidence of further activities by this organization which, for a brief period, loomed large in interprovincial educational activities.

Chapter 9

EDUCATIONAL RESEARCH

The CEA constitution, as amended and adopted in 1946, mentions as one of the four aims of the Association, "To foster educational research in Canada and Newfoundland and to publish reports of selected research studies."[1] The educational administrators who comprised in the main the continuing membership of the CEA have always professed a certain degree of interest in and respect for research. Except for the period from 1938 to 1943, however, it appears evident that the CEA's interest in research has on the whole been benevolent rather than active. The report of the Canadian Council for Educational Research (1939–1943) states that the establishment of a research council was discussed by the DEA in 1897,[2] 1901, and 1917. What was intended at the time was the establishment of a federal bureau of education which would serve as a national clearing house for information.[3] Since the collation of general information about Canadian educational statistics and practices would be basic to research, the DEA may be said, in this connection, at times to have held vigorous, though abortive, discussions directed towards research through the establishment of a federal bureau. Failing this, the CEA played a central role in the establishment of the Education Division of the Dominion Bureau of Statistics which was limited to the basic, but fundamental, area of statistics.

The importance of basic statistics was emphasized in the DEA as early as 1898 by Dr. J. M. Harper of Quebec, who argued that

[1]CEA *Constitution*, 1946, Appendix A.
[2]This should be 1898 since the DEA did not meet in 1897.
[3]See Chapter 7.

a bureau at Ottawa would be valuable for "securing greater uniformity and accuracy in school statistics, and so interpreting them that they may be more widely available and reliable as educational tests and measures." The Education Statistics Branch of the Dominion Bureau of Statistics was established in 1919, and the first Dominion-Provincial conference was held in 1920.[1]

The more active interest of the CEA in research dates from the seventeenth convention in Regina, October, 1936. At that time, Miss Jessie Norris, representing the Canadian Teachers' Federation, proposed that the CEA and the Canadian Teachers' Federation co-operate in promoting research;[2] this proposal was agreed upon as a course of action. Discussion followed as to whether the research program should be carried on by a central council which, working in co-operation with the Education Statistics Branch in Ottawa, would provide educational information and services and undertake some research, or by some other central office, limited to a director and secretary, which, aided by national and regional committees, would engage in general educational research.

Although the CEA convention agreed that a co-operative effort in promoting research was desirable, the directors, at their meeting following the convention, instructed the secretary to notify those working towards a bureau of educational research that the CEA could not at that time place any funds at the disposal of the committee. Since the CEA's income for the two-year period 1934–36 consisted of $1500 from the provinces and $68.00 from membership fees, this was a not unreasonable caution.

None the less, interest was maintained during 1937, largely through the efforts of Dr. M. E. LaZerte, vice-president of the Canadian Teachers' Federation and Director of the School of Education at the University of Alberta, Dr. F. M. Quance, Dean of Education at the University of Saskatchewan, Dr. Peter Sandiford, of the Ontario College of Education, and Dr. H. F. Munro, CEA president. The Carnegie Corporation of New York provided a grant of $1500 to defray the cost of a meeting on educational research which was held on May 30, 1938, in Toronto under the chairman-

[1]For the CEA's role in this see page 31.
[2]See page 37.

ship of Dr. H. F. Munro. Attended by fifteen persons including Dr.
A. C. Lewis and Dr. M. E. LaZerte, president and vice-president
respectively of the Canadian Teachers' Federation, and Dr. J. E.
Robbins of the Education Division of the Dominion Bureau of
Statistics, the meeting came to several important decisions including
one that the CEA be asked at its next meeting to appoint the first
members of the proposed research council. The following recommendations were made and subsequently adopted at the CEA convention in Halifax on August 16, 1938:

> . . . that a Canadian Council for Educational Research
> be established with the following objects:
>
> (a) to promote by its own efforts or by co-operation
>   with existing bodies the cause of research and in-
>   vestigation in education in Canada;
>
> (b) to publish in full or in summary form all edu-
>   cational researches in Canada that the Council
>   may determine to be useful;
>
> (c) to make grants to assist in the carrying out of
>   any research or investigation approved by the
>   Council;
>
> (d) to assist other educational bodies in the selection
>   of students qualified to carry on educational re-
>   search either in Canada or elsewhere;
>
> (e) to take any action that in the opinion of the
>   Council will assist any educational research;
>
> and that if Newfoundland should desire to participate in
> this scheme for educational research, the name and objects
> of the Council be modified to permit of such participation.

The question of obtaining support for the Council, and of its
organization, was left to the CEA directors. The fact should not be
overlooked, however, that Dr. M. E. LaZerte, then president of the
Canadian Teachers' Federation, was present at the convention
with authority to place $500 of Canadian Teachers' Federation
funds at the disposal of the proposed research council.

On January 23 and 24, 1939, the CEA called a meeting in
Toronto for the purpose of organizing a Canadian Council for
Educational Research. It was agreed that the Council should have
seven members, chosen as follows: one each from British Columbia,
the Prairie Provinces, Ontario, Quebec, and the Maritimes, the
chairman of the Canadian Teachers' Federation Research Com-

mittee, and the chief of the Education Branch of the Dominion Bureau of Statistics. Dr. LaZerte was appointed chairman.

The minutes of that meeting stated that the Council would be directly responsible to the CNEA. It was further agreed that Dr. John E. Robbins should discuss with the Carnegie Corporation, on a forthcoming visit, the question of a grant, but that a formal approach should be left to the secretary of the CNEA, then Dr. J. G. Althouse.

As a result of these efforts, the Council was advised, on April 10, 1939, that the Carnegie Corporation would contribute $10,000 for a research program and administrative expenses, $5000 at once and $5000 a year later. With this grant, the Council was able to embark upon an active program; its object, according to its constitution, was "to take any action that in the opinion of the Council would assist any educational research." Local branches were established in British Columbia, Alberta and Saskatchewan, Manitoba, Ontario, Quebec, New Brunswick, and Nova Scotia and Prince Edward Island. Each of these seven so-called advisory committees was to have not more than ten members. There is little evidence, however, that these branches or committees were ever very active.

In many ways it was unfortunate for the Council that the beginning and principal period of its activities coincided with a devastating world war. The CNEA, which should have met in 1940, did not meet until 1941. On that occasion, its theme was not, as it might otherwise have been, the support and program of the Canadian Council for Educational Research, but the importance of education for citizenship. Research in public education is necessarily of secondary interest during war time. In addition, studies undertaken with the aid of Council grants were often interrupted and indefinitely postponed when the research worker became involved in some activity related to the prosecution of the war. None the less, by September 1, 1943, expenditures of $8662.39 had been made from total receipts to that date of $13,858.53. Of these expenditures, 81.8 per cent had been in grants-in-aid, twenty-seven such grants having been awarded.

The Council reported regularly at CNEA conventions, but with the progress of war, educational research was increasingly handicapped and interrupted. In 1942, the chairman, Dr. LaZerte, had reported that not as many studies were being completed as desired. Requests for grants continued to be received and approved, however, so that at the 1944 convention, the chairman reported to the CNEA that something must be done to increase the funds available. Aware of this situation, the directors, at their meeting immediately preceding this report, voted $2000 from CNEA funds to augment the Council's resources.

There were many activities under consideration in the CNEA during the years 1944–45. Some of these were fruitful and were to be further developed; others were temporarily useful; still others were inconsequential, though not so recognized at the time. Amid these various stirrings, the Canadian Council for Educational Research, with its goal of educational research for its own sake and the strain that it was likely to impose upon CNEA funds, may have been regarded with a certain impatience. Several of the directors were determined that the Association should at last take action along specific lines, and the president, Dr. Fletcher Peacock, and the secretary-treasurer, Dr. C. E. Phillips, were men of superior imagination and vigor. If money were not available for some traditional desirable purpose, it seemed reasonable to them that some new desirable purpose be found for which money might become available. Experience had already indicated that research studies such as *A Preliminary Analysis of Oral Reading Achievement, A Preliminary Study of Spelling Readiness,* and *The Rorshach Test Applied to a Group of Delinquents,* however commendable in themselves, were unlikely to be productive of new funds or even to be self-supporting. Thus it happened that the CNEA president and secretary made preliminary approaches to life insurance company officials to determine their interest in school health research, and to both industry and business to ascertain their interest in a survey of secondary school curricula. The response to these approaches was encouraging.

At an executive meeting in June, 1945, the president was able to report that the Canadian Life Insurance Officers' Association had voted a grant of $10,000 for the first year of what was to become a five-year research program in school health. A joint committee of the CNEA and the Canadian Public Health Association was set up to supervise the study, with the CNEA to administer the project. The CNEA president was appointed chairman, and the chairman of the Research Council was one of the Committee.

This, the first of two such projects, was to have important implications for the Council in as much as the CNEA was establishing and sponsoring an *ad hoc* well-financed research committee independent of its own research organization. On the one hand, it was obvious that the life insurance companies would have a greater interest, financial and otherwise, in a project partly sponsored by the Canadian Public Health Association, but, on the other hand, the Council might well feel that both its functions and its authority were being ignored.

Three months later, at a meeting in August, 1945, the dissatisfaction of the Canadian Council for Educational Research was brought to the attention of the CNEA executive and was rather summarily dealt with. While the wording of the executive minutes of the Association is usually conspicuous for its blandness, though the meaning is definite enough, the Council in this case was bluntly instructed (1) to vote $2000 for the projected research program if it wished to participate (failing which the CNEA would use the Council's grant for this purpose); (2) that other specific research projects financed in the same manner would probably be undertaken by the CNEA; (3) to purchase a duplicating machine for the CNEA office; and (4) that the whole question of educational research would be discussed as soon as possible at a joint meeting of the Council and the CNEA directors.

No convention was held that year, but the CNEA directors and several members of the Canadian Council for Educational Research met on November 19 and 20, 1945. The president expressed the hope that the CNEA would give leadership in educational research, both through its own expert staff and through special committees. Discussion then followed on educational research and on sources of funds for such research. As a result of this discussion, it was resolved:

> That the Canadian Council for Educational Research should be disbanded, and that in its place there should

be created a CNEA Research Council whose powers and duties should be defined by the directors of the CNEA and which would take over the unfinished work of the Canadian Council for Educational Research, and that the funds of the Canadian Council for Educational Research should revert to the CNEA.

A committee was appointed to draw up a constitution for the newly-formed CNEA Research Council, and this new constitution was adopted on the following day. At the same time, the hope was strongly expressed by several directors that before long the CNEA would employ a full-time research director. Meanwhile, the CNEA made available up to $1500 for payment of grants-in-aid which the Research Council might approve.

As a conciliatory gesture, one article in the new constitution provided that the Research Council nominate the director of any research project for which funds were secured *ad hoc* by the CNEA. A difficulty arose when, in the spring of 1947, the CEA had secured funds from business, industry, and labor for a four-year survey of secondary school education, and a special Canadian Research Committee on Practical Education, representative of these interests, was appointed. At the fall meeting of the Research Council, the chairman, Dr. J. A. Long, explained that he was present when the research director for the special research committee was interviewed, but he felt that he did not participate in any real sense in his appointment. Dr. C. E. Phillips explained that with outside interests providing the funds, no other procedure was possible at the time. The constitution was revised again to omit the clause concerning the nomination by the Council of a director for any *ad hoc* research project.

The meeting in 1947 marked perhaps the lowest ebb in the affairs of the Research Council. The CEA was sponsoring two research programs, one by the National Committee for School Health Research for five years (1945–50) at a total cost of $58,000, the other by the Canadian Research Committee on Practical Education for four years (1947–51) at a cost of some $65,000. The Council played a minor part in both these studies which had active committees with the financial resources to meet regularly and to employ staff.

Other developments were now taking place within the CEA which, while they fell short of producing the kind of educational research which the Council wished to promote, were none the less encouraging.

The 1946 convention had passed a resolution that the CEA establish a research department with a full-time research director. This was, and still remains, a pious hope. However, in 1946 and 1947 the president and secretary began to promote the idea of a CEA Information Service, financed by grants, in proportion to the number of their teachers, from urban school boards. By the year 1948, almost $3000 was obtained from these sources, and the sum has increased each year. With the clerical assistance these grants helped to provide, a news letter was first mimeographed beginning in November, 1946; in May, 1948, it was printed on a basis of nine issues a year. Periodic reports were prepared on subjects of special interest to school boards and departments of education, and sections of the CEA quarterly journal were devoted to articles on research.

In addition, the CEA made available annually from $1500 to $2000 (later reduced to $1100) for the awarding of grants-in-aid by the Council. While the amount appears relatively small, no application has as yet been rejected by the Council because of lack of funds. In 1948, it was reported that, since 1939 when grants-in-aid were first awarded under the Canadian Council for Educational Research, thirty-four studies had been completed, eight had been discontinued, and five were still in progress.[1] Desirable as such studies are, however, it must be recognized that the Council has always, and quite rightly, regarded its proper function as much more active and positive than the mere awarding of grants-in-aid.

In 1950, the Research Council was enlarged through an invitation to the Canadian Teachers' Federation to name a representative to the Council in order to permit better liaison with that important body.

The Research Council continued to meet regularly at the time of the CEA conventions and to report to the convention as a whole.

[1] One copy of each study was to be deposited in (a) the OCE Research Library, (b) the Education Division, Dominion Bureau of Statistics, and (c) with the Chairman of the Council (Dr. LaZerte). After 1947, this practice was discontinued and two copies were deposited in the CEA office.

An excellent summary of the CEA's recent activity in research is given by the Council chairman, Dr. J. A. Long, in his report to the CEA in 1952:

> If one wished to be reassured of the interest of the Canadian Education Association in educational research, one has but to recall the major research projects which the Association has sponsored, and which it has either directed or helped to direct. The cumulative weight of the evidence is very convincing. There was the work of the Survey Committee on Educational Needs in Canada, the work of the National Committee for School Health Research, the work of the Canadian Research Committee on Practical Education, and the work of the LaZerte Committee on the Status of the Teaching Profession. There was the Lord study on Nursing Education in Canada, and there is the present study by LaZerte and Lortie on the Articulation of the High School and the University. And now we are embarked upon the CEA-Kellogg Project. Although this project may not be designed primarily as a research undertaking, I shall be surprised if research does not serve a major purpose in carrying the program to a satisfactory completion.
>
> These enterprises, along with a number of others of lesser magnitude, have been under the sponsorship of the directors of the CEA. The Research Council has done much to stimulate these projects. Generally, I feel that the Council, by its very existence, and by having a place in the annual proceedings, serves as a sort of catalytic agent helping to keep alive and nourish an interest in research by the Association as a whole.
>
> A direct influence of the Research Council is exercised through the grants-in-aid which it administers. Over the years, an impressive amount of research has been conducted under these grants.

The most recent development in the Research Council has been its co-operation with the Canadian Teachers' Federation and the Association of French-Language Educators in the formation of the National Advisory Committee on Educational Research, which held its first meeting in Ottawa on November 16 and 17, 1953. The committee, as approved by the directors of the three organizations participating, agreed that each organization should continue its independent research and information service programs, and should meet annually for the purpose of:

(1) surveying and reviewing annually the research efforts in all fields of public education;

(2) eliminating any overlapping of research efforts;

(3) discovering research areas not touched by any group;

(4) suggesting projects on which joint action might be taken.

It was further agreed that each organization would be represented by two voting members and a third non-voting member, if such further representation were desired. Of these bodies, only the Canadian Teachers' Federation has a research director, and it is as yet too early to assess the value of this joint committee, though its purpose is commendable.

The CEA Research Council has been a continuing active body, and from time to time it has advised upon and commended the work of the CEA Information Service; none the less, the Council has repeatedly emphasized that its proper functioning is dependent upon having a full-time research director. Until the CEA is in a position to appoint such a person, and there is no evidence at present that it soon will be, educational research in the CEA will necessarily be of an *ad hoc* and informational nature.[1] Valuable as this may be, it falls short of the goal of general educational research, primarily for its own sake, which the Canadian Council for Educational Research, later the CEA Research Council, had set for itself.

---

[1]As a result of negotiations conducted in the spring of 1957, it appears certain that the CEA will receive funds from a Canadian corporation to fulfill a number of desired research functions.

Chapter 10

DEPARTMENTS OR SECTIONS IN
THE CEA

Practical steps to organize the Dominion Educational Association were taken at a meeting of "Canadian teachers in attendance upon the National Education Association convention" in Toronto in 1891; many of these teachers were also members of the Ontario Educational Association. Since the DEA was envisioned as a national organization of persons in all phases of education, and since the NEA and OEA were divided into various departments or sections, it seemed reasonable that the DEA should also be organized into departments. It made provision for seven departments: School Inspection, Normal and Training Schools, Elementary Schools including Kindergartens, Higher Education, Industrial Education, Art Education, and Music Education. The presidents or presiding officers of these departments were automatically directors of the Association. This departmental organization continued until 1918.

During the period 1892 to 1909 inclusive, DEA meetings were well attended, with members on occasion filling large halls. At the same time, meetings of departments were equally well patronized; at these sectional meetings, minutes were often kept and published in the Proceedings, well-prepared addresses were delivered, and discussions followed the addresses. Under these circumstances, it might appear that the DEA in general was flourishing and that the departments in particular were functioning satisfactorily.

To assume this is to forget the vast geographic extent of Canada and the inability of most people in education, especially in those days, to find the time and the money required to travel long distances. In the period 1892 to 1909, the DEA met successively in Montreal, Toronto, Halifax, Ottawa, Winnipeg, Toronto, and Victoria, generally in conjunction with a teachers' convention or, in the case of the 1895 meeting, jointly with the Ontario Educational Association. In this last instance, except for some felicitous exchanges of compliments, it is difficult to find much evidence that the DEA met at all. On the other occasions, meetings at the successive conventions were well attended but *except for a dozen or so senior officials, never by the same people.* Thus to elect officers of a department and to keep minutes became increasingly pointless and frustrating. What was a serious problem for the senior officials of the DEA itself and brought about an intensive analysis of the organization in 1909, was an insuperable difficulty for the departments in the DEA. For the 1913 and 1917 conventions, no meetings of departments were organized, and in 1918 their discontinuance was made official by a complete revision of the constitution.

For a good many years thereafter, the CEA was a small organization consisting largely of delegates from provincial departments of education, heads of teacher training colleges, and principals of large schools. So small was the number of delegates in attendance at conventions that the question of departmentalization did not arise; indeed, as mentioned by Dr. G. F. McNally, the convention could meet in an ordinary committee room. Following World War II, however, and the further reorganization of the CEA, there was a greatly enlarged attendance, and the problem of the formation of some departments, or of sections, as they are now referred to, has again arisen.

The 1944 convention of the CNEA in Toronto was attended by 246 members, and the next convention, in Edmonton, had an attendance of slightly more than 300. At the latter meeting, a resolution came forward from a discussion group on technical and commercial education, that the CEA set up a section primarily concerned with vocational education. The Resolutions Committee took the view that the CEA could not, as yet, begin to deal with the great variety of educational problems in this way, and refused to endorse the resolution. While this decision settled the immediate question, the proposal with respect to vocational education was one of a number of similar proposals that arose in the next ten years concerning various special fields of education. From time to time, CEA conference groups on visual education, vocational guidance, art education, teacher training, school supervision, and others have, not without good reasons, requested that provision be made for them to meet as part of, or in conjunction with, the CEA convention.

No simple solution has been found to this problem of sectionalism. Part of the problem arises from the CEA's fundamental purpose of promoting liaison in educational matters and the exchange of information. When departmental officials, say in vocational guidance, and other persons interested in this phase of education, have not had an opportunity to exchange ideas, the CEA arranges a conference for them as part of its annual convention. Such a meeting usually proves both stimulating and fruitful, and the group may be invited to meet a second year. Quite frequently, and not unnaturally, efforts are then made by the special groups to meet regularly at the time of the CEA convention. Such efforts have so far been resisted by the CEA directors and by their executive because of certain problems inherent in the proposal.

Thus, at the 1947 convention, it was proposed that the CEA directors "be requested to consider the possibility of creating subdivisions of this organization to meet the needs of special groups within the framework of the CEA." The directors agreed on the importance of giving groups with particular interests some special recognition, providing "sectionalism was not overemphasized at the expense of the study of education as a whole." It was therefore decided that special groups should meet when possible, and that the office of the CEA should be used as a point of contact. This solution has not proved very satisfactory, first because, when it was not possible to hold conferences (and it was not possible to hold them frequently), the stimulus of personal meetings was lost and, secondly, because the CEA office has such a small staff with energy spread thin over a large number of activities, that no special interest groups could receive much attention throughout the year.

These difficulties have been partly overcome in different ways in different cases. Supervisors and teachers in art education, beginning in 1951, were encouraged to meet at several CEA conventions; when the CEA discontinued these meetings, the group was sufficiently vigorous and ingenious to organize the Canadian Society for Education through Art, which held its first independent meeting in 1955. A second group, the directors of visual education, has been enabled to meet, beginning in 1951, as the CEA-National Film Board Advisory Committee.[1] Expenses for these meetings were first paid by the departments concerned, but subsequently the National Film Board met transportation expenses. Directors of radio education meet as an advisory committee to the School Broadcasts Division of the Canadian Broadcasting Corporation, also with expenses paid. The directors of curriculum have been meeting regularly at CEA conventions because it is felt that this is an area where exchange of information and ideas is particularly necessary and desirable.

One of the most active groups meeting under CEA auspices has been teacher training personnel. These officials have now organized, on an effective basis, in western, central, and Atlantic meetings, and their zeal and enthusiasm may have led the CEA executive to a more generous practice in authorizing repeated meetings as part of the CEA convention. A further group that has received more than the usual encouragement consists of the school inspectors or superintendents. Because of their special meetings as part of the CEA-Kellogg Project in Educational Leadership, the CEA has given practical encouragement and assistance to the organization of a Canadian Association of School Superintendents and Inspectors which meets at the time of, but is not technically part of, the CEA. This group was organized in September, 1951, at the time that representative school inspectors were brought together to participate in planning for the CEA-Kellogg Project.

With respect to sections generally, one basic problem for the CEA directors lies in the fact that most of those who wish to organize as groups are departmental employees. Since these employees (directors of curriculum, directors of vocational education, chief inspectors, etc.), travel on expense allowances, not too many

[1]This committee first had representation, not from each department, but as follows: British Columbia-Alberta, 1; Saskatchewan-Manitoba, 1; Ontario-Quebec, 1; Atlantic Provinces, 2. Its organization has now been revised with representation from each province.

can attend CEA conventions in any one year, so they must alternate. Nor, apart from expenses, can too many senior officials be absent from the departments at any one time. A second basic problem is that the directors do not wish the CEA to be sectionalized as, for instance, are the Ontario Educational Association and the National Education Association of the United States. It is felt that this country is too extended, and the number of officials too few, for CEA members to be split up into a large number of little groups. It is further believed that educational philosophy and practice is better understood by each group, and more effective, when members of any one speciality know something of, and participate in, the deliberations of persons with other specialities. For these reasons the directors encourage intermixing at conference groups and resist any strong tendencies towards rigid sectionalism.

One special group may be noted as an exception to those mentioned above. This is the group of urban superintendents, the only group other than deputy ministers who have relative freedom to organize and to travel to meetings. Urban, locally employed superintendents have given strong and continuous support to the CEA since 1946, and conferences of particular interest to them have frequently been held at CEA conventions. After correspondence with the CEA office, Dr. W. C. Lorimer, Superintendent of Winnipeg Schools, courteously and reasonably suggested to the CEA directors that urban superintendents might more often be consulted and given more responsibility for the selection and development of some topics at the convention. This was readily agreed to by the directors (Dr. Lorimer was himself a director), and it was suggested that the possibility of extending the convention by an extra day, for the convenience of special groups, might well be explored. This procedure was thought sensible, since many delegates travelled long distances, at considerable expense, to the meetings. An extra day was provided at the 1955 and 1956 conventions.

It is difficult to anticipate to what extent the occasional meetings of special groups and the provision of an extra day will serve to satisfy the demands of these special interest groups. As a general policy, the directors would like the CEA to be an organization whose members, having due regard to their special fields, will continue to see the educational process as a whole. Developments since 1946, while not entirely satisfactory to those favoring sections, have none the less provided a compromise in which the CEA remains a unitary organization reasonably sensitive to the interests and desires of those who feel that they are primarily concerned with some particular phase of education. The official policy of the CEA on this subject was well expressed by Dr. W. H. Swift in his presidential address to the CEA in 1955:

> As yet, the CEA is an organization of quite modest size and resources, and it would weaken it very much if groups withdrew from it, either wholly or in part.
>
> There is danger that any one group may become too specialized, or narrow in its outlook. It seems useful that its members should associate not only with those of similar interest but also with educators and others who have different interests and problems.
>
> Specialists can make useful contributions, from their own points of view, to subjects being discussed by other groups. The teacher-trainers, for example, may have useful observations for the curriculum personnel. We must avoid too much rigid compartmentalization.
>
> Most persons attending our convention come when their employers assist with, or cover, their expenses. There is a practical limitation here, in that departments and other employers are prepared to send delegations of modest size. A large number of sections hoping to have annual meetings would, we think, languish through lack of attendance.

Chapter 11

EDUCATIONAL LIAISON IN OTHER COUNTRIES

Two of the four aims of the Canadian Education Association as shown in the constitution are "to collect and make available to educators in Canada information on educational developments in this country and elsewhere," and "to function as a co-ordinating agency." What the CEA is to co-ordinate is not specified, but a further aim refers to the promotion of understanding of educational ideals as between the provinces. It may be assumed, therefore, that the CEA is expected to have special responsibilities in educational matters of concern to more than one province and especially in the matter of collection and dissemination of information.

When one further considers that about 80 per cent of the CEA's budget comes from provincial departments, that no election of directors is valid unless each province is represented, and that the departments jointly control its policies, it follows that the CEA has a special relationship to the autonomous departments of education for purposes of liaison and information on public education. Of equal importance is the fact that there is no other organization in Canada maintained out of public funds, either federal or provincial, for these purposes. The absence of any other agency, and the special position of the CEA in relation to the politically responsible departments of education, consequently involves the CEA, unofficially or perhaps even semi-officially, in a number of liaison and information activities which are handled in other countries by offices organized and staffed for these particular purposes.

Countries that have a unitary system of government, such as the United Kingdom, New Zealand, and France, have, of course, a central ministry of education which is a unifying and controlling authority. In a second group of countries, such as India and the Union of South Africa, elementary and secondary education is not centrally controlled, but has been reserved as the domain of the state or province. None the less, these and some other countries have a central Ministry of Education (India) or Ministry of Education, Arts, and Science (Union of South Africa) which has special responsibility for some areas of education (such as universities, technical education, special education). In addition to such special functions, these central ministries act as a co-ordinating agency for the individual state authorities and they also, as in the cases of the two countries just mentioned, often have advisory and consultative committees comprised in large part of representatives of the state authorities. The Union of Soviet Socialist Republics, although a Federation, also has a central Ministry of Education in addition to the Ministry in each Soviet Republic.

There is a third small group of countries, federal in organization, in which education is primarily, if not exclusively, a state responsibility; these have no central or federal ministry of education. Examples of these are Switzerland, the United States, and Australia; a brief account is given in this chapter of how these rather exceptional countries provide for educational liaison and the dissemination of educational information as between their respective autonomous (in education) states or cantons. Since Canada is a federal state without either a federal ministry or a federal office of education, it is of interest to keep the Canadian situation in mind.

SWITZERLAND

It is often remarked that Switzerland and Canada are the only two countries in the world which have neither a central ministry nor federal office of education. Switzerland, which is 16,000 square miles in area, compared with Canada's 3,000,000 square miles, and has a population of 4,750,000, is divided into 25 cantons. Since each canton is sovereign with respect to education, Switzerland has twenty-five education systems, varied in form but unified in purpose. An account of Swiss liaison methods is therefore of particular interest to Canada, which has ten systems of education, and two languages.

The Swiss federal government makes certain limiting provisions concerning education, such as that it shall be free and compulsory; it may also establish a university, aid vocational education, and give subventions for primary education. However, in all legal and practical ways, each canton is independent and autonomous, and the purpose of this account is to indicate how, if at all, these cantons co-operate in matters of common interest in education, especially as, in addition to their twenty-five educational systems, the Swiss have three official languages.

In spite of the diversity of their language and the unique historic development of each cantonal system, the cantons have a long record of co-operation in the exchange of information and ideas. In 1898, the Swiss organized the Swiss Standing Conference of Heads of Cantonal Departments of Education; its purpose is "to facilitate personal contacts and to study school problems, as well as educational problems arising in all cantons and concerning all Swiss children and young people." The Conference has a permanent secretariat and meets annually or oftener when considered necessary; its president changes each year, and he is habitually the head of the education department where the annual conference is being held.

Formerly, the secretary of the Conference was one of the cantonal directors of public education, appointed by his colleagues, and continuing to perform his regular duties as well as secretarial duties for the Conference. Since 1931, however, the secretary has devoted all his time to the work of the Conference and has no other duties. The secretary's office is financed by the cantons on a *pro rata* basis according to their population. At present, the secretary has no clerical assistance but "the duties of the secretary grow heavier all the time as the problems in education become more numerous and complicated, and as relations with UNESCO and with foreign countries have been extended. I have no doubt that the secretariat will be organized or reorganized on a completely new basis as soon as circumstances permit."[1]

In these and other ways the Conference bears striking resemblance to the CEA. For instance, it has no legal powers and its decisions are only effective in so far as they may voluntarily be applied in each autonomous canton. Like the CEA, the Conference sets up special committees which present reports which are regarded as having considerable value. Generally, this collaboration within the Conference "has led to the general application of successful projects without any infringement of the canton's sovereignty." The Conference maintains an information and documentation centre.

In other ways, procedure differs appreciably from that followed in Canada. The Conference is responsible for school statistics, a function of the Education Division of the Dominion Bureau of Statistics in Canada, and it also publishes some school texts. When Switzerland is represented at international educational meetings, the federal government appoints the delegation, but the Conference secretary is habitually included, although there is no legal basis for this practice.

THE UNITED STATES

In the United States, as in other countries described in this chapter, education is decentralized; local autonomy is a fundamental principle in its administration. Since the Constitution of the United States did not specifically mention education as one of the powers of the federal government, and since powers not so delegated to the federal government were reserved to the several states, education is primarily a state responsibility. This determination of responsibility for education was much less specific than in Canada where the British North America Act (in Section 93) clearly assigned the control of education exclusively to the provinces.

Since 1867, however, the United States has had a Federal Office of Education. The office in the beginning was small, con-

---

[1]This quotation and the preceding information about the secretary's appointment are taken from a letter from the secretary (M. Antoine Borel) to the CEA dated March 23, 1956.

sisting of a Commissioner of Education and three clerks, and was created by Congress only after considerable discussion and not a little dissension. The bill to establish such an office, or department as it was first called, was opposed on the grounds that it was unconstitutional, a waste of public money, and a dangerous step toward the centralization of education. It was particularly feared that the North would infringe the freedom and educational rights of the Southern States. On the other hand, Representative Ignatius Donnelly said, in part:

> While it (the Office) will have no power to enter into the states and interfere with their systems, it will be able to collect facts and report the same to Congress, to be thence spread over the entire country. It will throw a flood of light over the dark places of the land. It will arouse to increased activity the friends of education everywhere, and ignorance will fly before it.

This was a somewhat substantial assignment for a staff of four, but the United States Office of Education has since grown to be a large and influential factor in education in the United States. Financed by the federal government under the Secretary of Health, Education, and Welfare, the Office has a staff of some 500 employees and, for the fiscal year 1956, an appropriation for salaries and expenses of $3,050,000. In addition, the Office administers grants of $128,000,000 (vocational education, $34,000,000; higher education, $5,000,000; school assistance, $89,000,000). It has thus for a good many years been in a position to fulfil the hopes of its early promoters. The establishment of a federal office had been strongly urged by educationists from 1840 to 1867 and was a subject at almost every national educational meeting of any importance. These educationists wanted an office to promote the exchange of educational information among the states, to publish a journal, and to report on educational progress in the United States and elsewhere.

The United States Office of Education was fortunate in the choice of its first Commissioner of Education, Henry Barnard. Barnard was enthusiastic and industrious and had had extensive experience as an educationist, administrator, editor, author, and scholar. None the less, the Office had difficulties in its first years.

Appointed as Commissioner in 1867 at a salary of $4000 (a member of Congress received $3000), Barnard had his salary reduced the following year to $3000 under a Secretary of the Interior who was unfavorably disposed towards the Office. The Office received more encouragement under a new secretary in 1870, and Barnard, who resigned as Commissioner in that year, was succeeded by John Eaton, who remained in office for sixteen years.

The early work of Henry Barnard and his successor gave the Office broad scope for the future. Apparently there was no intention, either in its creation or operation, to limit its functions and service, except that it was not to control education; that function was to remain with the individual states.

In view of the functions and growth of the United States Office of Education, it is understandable that many Canadian educationists, especially from 1892 to 1917, relied heavily upon its publications and hoped for the establishment of a similar office in their own country. The present activities of the Office of Education are literally too numerous to mention. However, in spite of its enlargement, the Office still has no administrative authority over public education in state or local school systems. "Its functions are statistical, informational, and advisory, except as provided by special Acts of Congress for the provision of financial assistance to states and local communities." More specifically, its purposes have been summarized in a report of the United Nations Educational, Scientific, and Cultural Organization as follows:

> To collect, interpret, and distribute educational information on all levels and in all fields of education; to carry on research and publish the results; and the wide range of activities related to these functions. (The Office holds various administrative responsibilities including administration of certain federal funds for educational purposes such as those for vocational education, land grant colleges, and universities; administrative assistance in the program for the international exchange of teachers; and for other programs authorized from time to time.)

The Office of Education also has special responsibilities, as might be expected, in representing the United States at international educational conferences. An official from the Office attends the United Nations Educational, Scientific, and Cultural Organization–International Bureau of Education annual International Conference on Public Education in Geneva as one of a three-member delegation appointed and with expenses paid by the State Department. A state school system official is usually a second member. The Office is also represented on the delegation which the United States government sends to UNESCO's Biennial Conference, usually, but not necessarily, by the Commissioner serving as the vice-chairman of the delegation.

AUSTRALIA

The Commonwealth of Australia, where education is also primarily a state concern, was the most recent of the three federal countries under review to establish at public expense an office for educational liaison and information. The Commonwealth Office of Education was created by Act of Parliament in 1945 and attached to the Prime Minister's department of the Commonwealth government; it is financed entirely from government funds. Since 1945 the central office in Sydney has been expanded by the establishment of four branch offices located in Melbourne, Brisbane, Adelaide, and Perth.

The functions of the Commonwealth Office were originally stated to be:

1. to advise the Minister on matters relating to education;
2. to establish and maintain liaison on matters relating to education, with other countries and with the states;
3. to arrange consultation between Commonwealth of Australia authorities concerned with matters relating to education;
4. to undertake research relating to education;
5. to provide statistics and information relating to education required by any Commonwealth of Australia authority;
6. to advise the Minister concerning the grant of financial assistance to the states and to other authorities for educational purposes, and to undertake such other functions in relation to education as are assigned to it by the Minister.

Since then, the Office has assumed increased responsibility for native education and for the education of the large influx of immigrants to that country. Following the recent world war, interest has greatly intensified in various countries respecting the educational ideas and practices of other countries. This interest has been extended through the creation and work of UNESCO, and in these matters the Australian Office has played a prominent part within that country.

While in the United States the Department of the Secretary of State provides the secretariat for the United States National Commission, in Australia this secretariat is provided by the Commonwealth Office which also acts in an executive and advisory capacity in connection with Australia's membership in UNESCO. The assistant director of the Office headed the Australian delegation to UNESCO's Biennial Conference in Montevideo in 1954, and the briefing of the delegation, it is interesting to note, was undertaken by the Office in conjunction with the Department of External Affairs. The Office also advised on the selection of participants and the preparation of reports for a wide variety of conferences and seminars.

It may be seen that the recently created Commonwealth Office has been increasingly active as a liaison and information centre in education; in fact, the Office itself reports that "the Commonwealth Government has been brought more and more into the field (of education)."

A further central agency is also active in Australian education— the Australian Council for Educational Research, located in Melbourne. Established in 1930, with financial assistance for a ten-year period from the Carnegie Corporation of New York, it should be mentioned in this context because it is now financially supported by the Commonwealth government and by six state governments, although it retains its autonomy. Grants from Commonwealth and state governments amounted, for the fiscal year ending June 30, 1954, to £10,000 (Australian £ = $2.24 United States). Teachers' associations contributed about £190 and private business firms £1000.

With a staff of twenty (thirteen professional, seven clerical), the Council, as its name suggests, is primarily concerned with research; it makes grants to approved investigators and publishes reports useful to the teaching profession. More specifically, and quite reasonably, it would appear that the Council is particularly interested in tests and measuring devices in the educational and psychological fields and in the dissemination of research findings rather than in liaison and administration in education.

However, it is of considerable interest in this present study that the Council, as a central agency in educational research, is supported in a federal state largely by contributions from both federal and state funds.

PART III

The Canadian Education Association
Since 1948

Chapter 12

WHAT *IS* THE CANADIAN EDUCATION ASSOCIATION?

The writer was once told that the Germans, when they invaded France in the Franco-Prussian War, were much puzzled by the small windows they observed over the doorways leading into rooms; they had not seen such windows before. This window, known in English as a transom, frequently prompted the question "Was ist das?" and for a while it was popularly called by the Germans a "Was-ist-das" — what is that?

"What is it?" is a question regularly asked about the CEA by foreign educational visitors to its office, for they find it a puzzling and unfamiliar kind of organization. A reply requires an explanation of Canada's federal structure and some brief remarks on the constitutional autonomy of the ten provincial education departments. Canada, it is pointed out, is the only country in the world, except Switzerland, having neither a national ministry of education nor a federal office of education; therefore the provincial departments of education maintain the CEA voluntarily as an informal liaison office. What is the role of a voluntary informal office when it is called upon, not by right but by lack of any other instrument for the purpose, to do necessary and official tasks? The CEA's position in such matters is a peculiar one; in certain respects, its status with the provinces is that of a common-law wife, involving the accompanying embarrassment that such a relationship might be expected to occasion.

Apart from its functions as a hand-maiden (and a shy one) of the provincial departments, the CEA is secondly an educational association to which anyone (who is engaged in education in its broadest sense) may belong, on payment of a membership fee of $2.00. This $2.00 membership fee, still only double what it was in 1892, does not cover the actual cost of printing and mailing the CEA's quarterly magazine, *Canadian Education,* to which each individual member is entitled. In consequence, each new member of the CEA, far from being a source of income to the organization, is an actual expense to it. As an association, then, the CEA is an organization which could not continue to survive for long if it were dependent on members' fees.

Thirdly, the CEA maintains an Information Service for a large number of urban school systems which pay grants of fifty cents per classroom under the jurisdiction of the board. Forty-two boards participated in 1955, providing $6692. The CEA provides a printed *News Letter* (nine issues a year), periodic mimeographed reports, and special reports on request to members of the Information Service.

In considering the CEA's role, it is necessary to recognize from the outset that "he who pays the piper calls the tune." The income for the CEA's operating budget in 1955 was $43,489.47, of which $33,757.50 came from the provinces in grants proportionate to their population; $6692.00 came from urban school boards in proportion to the number of their classrooms; and $1922.20 was derived from membership fees and subscriptions to the magazine. The percentage of support from these three sources in round figures is: provincial departments of education 80 per cent; urban school boards 15 per cent; and membership fees and magazine subscriptions 5 per cent. This dependence of the CEA on the provincial departments was described by one CEA president, Dr. W. H. Swift, with some degree of understatement, as follows: "While the Association in its membership and interests has diverse connections, it does have a rather special relationship to the provincial departments of education."

Thus it would appear that the CEA is a voluntary organization which is maintained primarily by the departments of education, receiving some financial assistance from local school authorities, and to which any educationist may belong on payment of a nominal membership fee.

The CEA, viewed only as another voluntary education association, one of some sixty or seventy national associations, would be
like Hamlet without the Prince of Denmark. Such a view would
ignore the long history of the CEA outlined in Part I, and particularly the repeated efforts to establish a central office of education,
either under federal or interprovincial control, outlined in greater
detail in Chapter 7. It would ignore provisions made in other
countries for the internal dissemination of educational information
and particularly for the exchange of educational information among
different countries.

Not everyone would go as far, in appraising the special position
of the CEA, as Dr. B. O. Filteau, who retired in 1955 as Deputy
Minister of Education in Quebec after fifty years of service in education. For thirty years Dr. Filteau attended almost every meeting
of the CEA. In 1955 he described the establishment, in 1945, of the
CEA office as "a definite and satisfactory solution to the critical and
oftentimes discussed question of the establishment of a federal
bureau of education. Instead of a federal bureau," said Dr.
Filteau, "it was unanimously agreed, after long discussion, to
establish an interprovincial bureau under the direction of a full-
time executive secretary." While these are strong statements, great
weight must be attached to them, because of Dr. Filteau's long
experience and his position in a province reputedly more opposed
to centralization than any others. The fact is that there are an
appreciable number of educational activities in a federal country
which need to be undertaken by some central education office. The
CEA has been called upon to undertake, however unofficially,
many of these activities. The performance of these activities has had
a significant effect upon the role of the CEA as a voluntary
organization.

AN ORGANIZATION OF EDUCATIONISTS

It will be recalled that the CEA began as an organization of educationists for the purpose of exchanging ideas and advancing the
cause of education. Originally modelled largely on the National
Education Association and the Ontario Educational Association,

and composed of teachers, principals, teacher-training personnel, inspectors and other provincial officials, organized into various departments, the CEA met in conjunction with provincial teachers' associations. Its conventions were large, enthusiastic, and hopeful, but, since there was no continuity of the membership at large nor provision for activity between conventions, the motion was up and down rather than forward.

The early records seem to indicate that the CEA was thought of as serving two purposes: (1) enabling teachers (the word was then used as loosely and inclusively as educationist now is) to meet, listen to learned addresses by senior officials, exchange ideas, establish personal contacts, and renew their educational faith, and (2) organizing opinion in support of a federal bureau of education. Distance, with the accompanying expense of travel, defeated the former; the attitude of several of the provinces defeated the latter. With its reorganization, proposed in 1917 and effected in 1918, into a small representative body, the CEA did not again serve, until its further reorganization in 1946, as a general educational association.

Increasingly since 1946, the CEA convention has provided a general meeting ground for persons interested in all aspects of education, apart from university education; teacher education at the university level, of course, receives particular attention at the convention. The convention provides the only opportunity for such persons to meet. In regular attendance at the annual CEA convention may be found eight of the ministers of education, since usually one or two are prevented by business of office or pressing engagements from attending, all the deputy ministers of education, from each province several directors of divisions within a department, a representative number of school inspectors, the directors of education of major urban school systems, large numbers of representatives of textbook publishing houses, representatives of the provincial associations of teachers and the Canadian Teachers' Federation, a substantial number of school trustees from all provinces, and representatives of the home and school movement.

Attendance at the CEA convention varies from 350 to 500 persons, including wives of delegates; from 300 to 400 of those in attendance are actual delegates. Since all provinces are pretty well represented in proportion to population, the convention is truly national and thus much different from the large conventions from 1892 to 1909.[1] In its role as a general education organization, the CEA, at its convention, serves as a national forum at which all aspects of education can be freely discussed.

Apart from its convention, and the circulation of its quarterly magazine, the CEA office has little contact with association members throughout the year, except through carrying out certain of its other activities which are described below. Nor do the individual members, unless they are also representative delegates, have the right to vote on resolutions or other expressions of policy of the Association.

AN INFORMATION CENTRE

Sir Winston Churchill made famous his statement, "Give us the tools and we will finish the job." It is perhaps pertinent to suggest that Dr. Fletcher Peacock acted on the somewhat reverse policy, "Give us (the CEA) the job and we will find the tools." This intriguing method of operation is shown in the initiation in 1946 of the CEA's Information Service.

One of the most fruitful post-war activities undertaken by the CEA was the provision of the Information Service for urban school boards. As stated above, twenty school boards contributed about $3000 in 1946–47 towards the maintenance of an Information Service by the CEA. By 1955, membership had grown to forty-two boards which subscribed $6692.

Insufficient in itself to provide for the service, the amount supplements other revenues so that the CEA can employ additional staff and publish special reports and a *News Letter*. These contain information primarily of interest to urban school officials. Regular reports are prepared on such matters as teachers' and administrators' salaries, school enrolment, teacher certification, and a directory of administrative officials, while special reports are prepared on school cafeterias, functions of school boards, safety education, salaries of

[1]See pages 17 and 19.

clerical employees, and other matters on request of one or more boards.

The CEA sends to each participating board copies of the *News Letter* in sufficient quantities for board members, administrative officials, and school principals. *Canadian Education* and special reports are sent in enough copies for board members and administrative officials. All such material is sent in bulk to the director of education or secretary-treasurer of the board for his further distribution.

The CEA *News Letter* also receives special distribution through departments of education. Not only is it distributed to a limited extent within each department, but the department itself sends copies to all provincially employed inspectors, who at present number 690. The total circulation of an issue of the *News Letter* is now 2900 copies.

Because of its special contacts with and work for the departments of education, the CEA has at hand in summary form considerable information of interest to local school authorities. Conversely, because of its contacts with and work for these local authorities, the CEA is also able to make available to all education departments interesting information on local school practices in various parts of the country. Departments of education and local school authorities have designated specific officials who are expected to keep the CEA informed of new developments and interesting activities in education for use in the *News Letter* and in special reports.

Through the above methods there is an interaction of forces which the CEA can direct to the benefit of all concerned. At the same time as the CEA assembles information on education, it is becoming more widely known as a central source of such information. In consequence, the Association's office receives many enquiries some of which it has neither the staff nor resources to answer with any degree of competence. Many individuals and agencies within Canada, and most enquirers from outside Canada, are interested in information on such matters as curriculum, teacher training, salaries, school board functions, school buildings, with reference to Canada as a whole rather than with reference to any one province. To the extent that it can, the CEA provides such information. When it cannot, the CEA none the less still serves a very useful purpose in directing the enquirer to the best or most convenient source of information within a particular province. Although the Information Service of the CEA is far from being fully developed, it holds possibilities of great value to Canadian education.

A SPONSOR OF SPECIAL STUDIES

The CEA's operating budget, particularly in the years 1945–48, was exceedingly small. Two factors, however, render misleading an estimate of the Association's effectiveness based on its budget alone. One is the opportunity that the CEA has, as an office supported by the departments of education and a large number of school boards, of enlisting the co-operation in a given activity of these well-staffed and resourceful authorities. The other factor is the opportunity that the CEA has, as an informal central education office with a secure budget for operating expenses, of obtaining financial support for specific projects from commercial and industrial enterprises and from Foundations. Once the CEA had established an office, its small staff made considerable use of both these factors.

Mention has already been made[1] of the report of the Survey Committee. Among its recommendations for the improvement of post-war education were greater attention to health in the school and greater variety in the courses available in secondary schools.

A successful approach was made by the CEA to the Canadian Life Insurance Officers' Association for funds to support a study of school health problems. In consequence, the CEA established the National Committee for School Health Research; this was a joint committee with the Canadian Public Health Association for the purpose of supervising the study, each organization being represented by four members. Office space was provided in the CEA offices, with the CEA also providing the administrative arrangements for the program.

[1]See page 45.

The Committee's budget was $10,000 for the first year and $12,000 for each of the four years following (September 1945 to September 1950); the Committee was thus able to employ a research director, Dr. A. J. Phillips, a secretary-stenographer, and to meet expenses of travel, publications, and committee meetings. With the co-operation of provincial departments of education and of health, advisory committees were established in each province.

Printed publications of the Committee were *A Health Survey of Canadian Schools, Some Data on Mental Health Problems, Absenteeism in Canadian Schools* (15,323 pupils, Grades I to XIII in representative schools for one year), a condensation of the elaborate absenteeism study, and *An Aid to Better School Housekeeping.* A summary of the project, entitled *A Five-Year Program in School Health Research* was also printed. A report on teacher training in health was mimeographed. A special study was made, in the Clover Bar School Division, Alberta, of the value of the course in preventive medicine designed for teachers; this was published in summary form in *Canadian Education* in September, 1949. An interesting subsequent development, also financed by the Canadian Life Insurance Officers' Association, was the production of a film based on the Committee's work, entitled *Our School Children's Health.*

A second major project sponsored by the CEA was a survey in the field of secondary education. The Canadian Research Committee on Practical Education was established with the support of, and in co-operation with, the Canadian Manufacturers' Association, the Canadian Chamber of Commerce, the Canadian Teachers' Federation, labor unions, and other bodies for the purpose of making a study of the practicality of the secondary school program for students proceeding directly to employment. The Committee, which consisted of one representative each of the various contributing organizations, elected an executive board of twelve members, six of whom (by the Committee's constitution) were named by the CEA.

As in the case of the School Health Committee, Dr. Fletcher Peacock was chairman until his death in January, 1949. Office space for the Committee's staff, and administration were again provided by the CEA. The Committee had a paid staff from August 1947 to July 1951, first consisting of a research director, Mr. A. G. McColl, and a stenographer, and subsequently, from the spring of 1949, a research assistant also.[1] Similar to the organization of the work of the School Health Committee, provincial advisory committees were established in each province.

Printed publications of the Committee were *Practical Education in Canadian Schools* (March, 1949), *Your Child Leaves School* (March, 1950), *Two Years After School* (March, 1951), and *Better Schooling for Canadian Youth* (September, 1951). In addition there were a number of mimeographed reports.

During its four years of existence, the Committee received $66,000 from fifty-seven contributors; the largest amounts came from the following organizations: The Canadian Bankers' Association ($5500), the Canadian Chamber of Commerce ($8000), the Canadian Congress of Labor ($7500), and the Canadian Manufacturers' Association ($8500). The average yearly budget for the project was thus $16,500. As distinct from the National Committee for School Health Research, expenses of members of the Committee and of the executive board were paid by their employers and not by the project budget.

Many of the publications of the National Committee for School Health Research and of the Canadian Research Committee on Practical Education were first printed in *Canadian Education* as well as reprinted for these Committees, and are readily available, together with comments about them, in CEA publications and elsewhere.

At the request of the ministers of education attending the CEA Convention in Quebec in September, 1947, the directors established a committee of five persons under the chairmanship of Dr. M. E. LaZerte[2] to make a study of the status of the teaching profession. The committee reported at the convention the next September and recommended that a new committee be established to develop a program of action to improve the conditions indicated in the report.

[1]Until the fall of 1950 this was Mr. J. A. Keddy, who was succeeded by Mr. J. D. Ayers.
[2]Other members were Dr. F. S. Rutherford, Mr. H. P. Moffatt, Mr. George Croskery, and Mgr A. M. Parent.

The report of the new committee, made in September, 1949, and entitled *Recommendations Concerning the Status of the Teaching Profession,* became one of the most widely read documents in Canadian education. Two thousand copies were published in *Canadian Education,* December, 1949, and a special reprint was made of a further 2000 copies; only 100 copies of this report were undistributed by the spring of 1950, and numerous requests were made for it long after it was out of print. The new Committee on the Teaching Profession, also under the chairmanship of Dr. M. E. LaZerte[1], made forty-four recommendations (distributed as indicated by the figures shown in brackets) under such headings as "Selection and Training of Teachers" (20), "Teacher Supply and Demand" (3), "The Economic Status of Teachers" (7), "Living and Working Conditions" (8), and "Teaching as a Profession" (6).

The work of the committee on the Status of the Teaching Profession is an impressive illustration of the ability of the CEA to obtain the voluntary services of senior educationists in carrying out a large project without expense to the Association. Involved in this undertaking were scores of educational administrators, teacher-training personnel, and teachers, yet there was no paid staff, save for some editorial services provided by the CEA office.

A much more modest study, but also involving a national survey, was one on the articulation of high schools and universities. Also undertaken by Dr. LaZerte, on behalf of the CEA, in co-operation with Dr. Leon Lortie, representing the National Conference of Canadian Universities, a study was made of the requirements for high school leaving certificates in all the provinces and of the requirements of all Canadian universities for entrance into their various faculties. A condensation of this study is contained in *Canadian Education* for September, 1952.

The most ambitious of the special projects undertaken by the CEA has been the CEA-Kellogg Project in Educational Leadership. The origin of the project is partly related to the fact that the CEA, from its establishment of an office in 1945, has, at any given time, been sponsoring one or more special projects of the kind

[1]Other members were Mr. Charles Bilodeau, Mr. George Croskery, Mr. H. P. Johns, Mr. H. P. Moffatt, Dr. C. E. Phillips.

described above. One of these, the School Health Committee, completed its work in 1950, and another, the Practical Education Committee, in 1951. The CEA executive secretary was therefore requested by the executive to discuss with Foundations in the United States the possibility of obtaining funds for educational research; some areas for such research were outlined. The W. K. Kellogg Foundation was approached, and Dr. R. G. VanDuyn of that Foundation visited the CEA office in April, 1951. He made it clear that his Foundation was not interested in research projects but might be willing to discuss some sort of action program.

Being aware that the establishment of the larger unit of school administration was one of the most significant post-war developments in Canadian education, the secretary suggested that a study be made of the problems arising from this development. As he was himself a member of a school board which had recently replaced thirteen smaller boards, the secretary had some first-hand knowledge of such a board's problems. In addition, Dr. J. G. Althouse, Ontario's Chief Director of Education, had asked the CEA secretary that spring if he would arrange for some Ontario inspectors to exchange ideas with western inspectors on problems in the administration of larger school areas.

Discussions with Dr. VanDuyn for a project with Canadian school superintendents in the field of school supervision and administration proved fruitful. A detailed program was subsequently worked out by the CEA, receiving Foundation approval in December, 1951, for an amount of $230,282 over the five-year period January 1, 1952, to December 31, 1956. As it developed, the Foundation was sufficiently satisfied with the success of the program, somewhat revised for the last two years, to make a total of $266,000 available to the CEA.

Since the average yearly amount of the assistance sought was considerably in excess of the CEA's budget, a project of this substantial nature could have had several effects, not all of them desirable, on the welfare of the CEA as an organization. As this project, apart from the establishment of the CEA office, has had more influence on the recent activities of the CEA than any other, certain internal problems should be noted here.

An astute observer with an analytical mind, Dr. VanDuyn was well aware that a very large Foundation grant might throw the CEA, so to speak, off balance. He was also of the opinion that the CEA needed financial support and general strengthening to fill the vacuum in Canadian education existing through the lack of any other central educational agency. On the other hand, the CEA had sponsored two major studies which, under their committee names, had become widely known while the CEA remained relatively unknown. In fact, one research director complained that his work was handicapped because the CEA as an organization was largely unknown to principals and teachers. With reference to the special studies, the CEA executive secretary had kept minutes and paid expenses, but in each case the research director felt responsible to his special committees, not to the CEA. Partly to overcome this separation as revealed by the work of the School Health Committee in its early operations, Dr. C. E. Phillips, shortly before his resignation became effective, drafted a constitution for the Practical Education Committee, making its research director responsible to the CEA secretary between committee meetings. This latter arrangement was only partly effective and the two *ad hoc* committees were not too closely identified with the CEA. In theory, "these two committees were created by the CEA,"[1] and "it was always understood that the CEA secretary was the executive officer of these organizations,"[1] but this understanding, though any issue over the situation was carefully avoided, was not entirely shared by the research directors. Thus it happened that the National Committee on School Health Research and the Canadian Research Committee on Practical Education (quite temporary committees) became rather widely known, while the CEA, which was completely responsible for their initiation and largely responsible for their programs, gained relatively little in prestige and publicity beyond a limited circle.

Working from quite different points of view, but towards the same end—the enhancement of the prestige of the CEA and its development as an effective agency—the Foundation representative and the CEA secretary planned the new project as an integral part

[1]CEA, Minutes of the Executive Committee, November 29, 1948, Dr. Peacock, page 4.

of the CEA rather than as a CEA-sponsored semi-autonomous activity. The project has met with general success and approval, and in consequence the Kellogg Foundation has made a further commitment of $70,000 to the CEA for the expansion of its activities over the four-year period from January 1, 1957, to December 31, 1960. A commitment of $127,000 over the same period has been made to the University of Alberta, which co-operated with the CEA in a series of three-week short courses for school inspectors, for an expanded graduate program in school supervision and administration.

Considerable credit for the success of this project and for these further developments is due to Dr. G. E. Flower, its program director, who has shown both unique skill in administration and firm and enthusiastic support of the CEA as an agency for the advancement of Canadian education.

AN INTERPROVINCIAL EDUCATION OFFICE

On page 113, Dr. B. O. Filteau was quoted as saying that the establishment of the office of the CEA offered a solution to the question of the establishment of a federal bureau of education. It is doubtful if it would be generally agreed that the CEA offers a satisfactory solution. However, it might well be agreed that, because of a lack of a national office, the CEA is called upon to undertake a number of activities with which an association is not usually concerned and which would more naturally be the re-sponsibility of an interprovincial or central office of education. Because of this situation, the CEA often functions as such an office.

Taking note of the difficulties in the way of a federal office, Dr. C. E. Phillips has asked what type of organization might be acceptable to all the provinces and able to perform most of the functions expected of a federal office. In reply to his own question, he suggests, "A voluntary organization supported by the provincial educational authorities; that is, the CEA."[1]

In view of the opinions just quoted, one from an experienced administrator and the other from an educational historian and

[1]See Chapter 15.

philosopher, it is important to note some of the activities of the CEA in its function as an interprovincial office.

A number of instances have been given in the earlier history of the association where the CEA acted or spoke on behalf of the provincial departments of education. The earliest example of this was the approval of Empire Day;[1] another was the CEA's endorsement of an education branch in the Dominion Bureau of Statistics. Considerable attention was also given to the need for federal support for agricultural and technical education. Under the pressure of World War II there were many occasions on which the Association acted for the departments, the most notable example being the establishment of the Survey Committee in 1942 and the impressive report of that Committee in the following year. According to Dr. J. G. Althouse, one "momentous result" was that "the Association spoke for Canadian education with surprising authority and unanimity."[2] Also during the war, the CEA approved the National Advisory Committee on School Broadcasting and assessed, on behalf of the provinces, the extensive education courses offered by Canadian Legion War Services Incorporated.

Immediately following the war, the CEA was most active in attempting to obtain certain war assets which were urgently needed for use in the schools. All provinces except Quebec authorized the CEA Secretary to act on their behalf in this matter.

An interesting case history of the CEA's function as an agency for the provincial departments of education is provided in the problem of the education of new Canadians following World War II. In 1947, when this problem first became acute, the Citizenship Branch of the Department of the Secretary of State asked the CEA directors to suggest a basic syllabus for post-school education of immigrants. The directors agreed to appoint a committee which would draw up and recommend such a syllabus for approval by the respective provinces. The syllabus was subsequently adopted by virtually all the provinces. The CEA continued for a time to be active on behalf of the provinces on matters pertaining to the education of new Canadians, for an interesting constitutional

[1]See page 16.
[2]See Chapter 15.

question was involved. Immigration was a federal responsibility as was the naturalization or certification of immigrants as Canadian citizens. The training or education for such citizenship, however, was a provincial responsibility, and the Canadian government has always been zealous in avoiding the appearance of interfering with education. The problem was further complicated by the fact that members of the judiciary were responsible for deciding whether or not an immigrant was qualified for Canadian citizenship, and the federal government felt that it could not instruct judges in this responsibility. Thus the provinces were not able to obtain from the Canadian government a statement of what an immigrant was expected to know, and thus should be taught, in order to qualify for Canadian citizenship.

In this comic opera setting, the CEA secretary carried on many discussions and prepared numerous memoranda; and to the credit of all concerned satisfactory arrangements were made. Gradually, at the request of the CEA on behalf of the provinces, the federal government produced a series of special booklets for free use by the provinces in the education of immigrants. As liaison between federal and provincial authorities in this field improved, accompanied by a growth of confidence in the good intentions of both parties, the CEA withdrew as an intermediary agency. One of the CEA's last official visits to the federal department at the ministerial level was to press for direct financial aid for evening classes in language and citizenship; although refused at the time, this aid was granted two years later in 1953.

The significance of the CEA's action in this illustration lies in its role as an agency of the provinces, its freedom as an intermediary to propose and discuss matters in an informal way, and its readiness to withdraw from the scene when its services were no longer essential to the promotion of an activity.

Generally speaking, it might be assumed that the CEA is primarily an agency for the provincial departments of education, since the latter provide more than three-quarters of its budget. The senior educational official of each department is always a member of the Board of Directors, and the deputy ministers constitute a majority of the Board's executive committee. Though the ten provinces are completely autonomous in their control of education and the CEA by its constitution supports this situation, there are quite a few occasions on which it is desirable and even necessary for the regularly constituted authorities to work together. Under these circumstances, the CEA is an invaluable agency for them, and if the CEA did not exist, it would probably be necessary to invent such an organization.

Many countries carry on a teacher-exchange program. The United States does so through the United States Office of Education, the United Kingdom through the League of the Commonwealth and Empire acting on behalf of the Ministry of Education, France through its Ministry of Cultural Affairs. Both for exchanges with other countries and between provinces within Canada, the CEA acts officially on behalf of the provinces. During 1955–56 there were forty-six exchanges with the United Kingdom,[1] four with the United States, and ten teachers were on exchange between provinces in Canada. Currently, an experiment is being made in arranging two exchanges with the New Zealand Department of Education, and the Canadian interchange program itself has recently been expanded to include teacher-training and supervisory personnel as well as classroom teachers.

On several occasions, the CEA has selected one outstanding high school student to be a guest in that country of the government of Brazil; it has also selected, by interprovincial agreement, groups of fifty high school students to be guests of a Canadian industrialist[2] on an extended tour of the United Kingdom.

By agreement among the provinces, the CEA has, for the past few years, prepared brief annual reports of approximately three thousand words on developments in education, as well as reports on two special educational topics, different each year, for the International Conference on Public Education, Geneva. Sponsored jointly by the International Bureau of Education in Geneva and the United Nations Educational, Scientific, and Cultural Organization, the conference is attended by representatives of some fifty countries. While Canada is not a member of the International Bureau of Edu-

---

[1] Reduced for that year only from the customary number of 55 to 46.
[2] Mr. Garfield Weston.

cation, it is expected to participate in the conference as a member of the United Nations Educational, Scientific, and Cultural Organization.

Prior to 1950, Canada was occasionally represented at the Geneva conference by a junior member of a Canadian embassy staff or by some Canadian educationist who happened by coincidence to be in the area at the time of the conference. This casual arrangement was hardly an appropriate way to provide representation at an international conference having considerable prestige. The CEA therefore proposed to the ministers of education, meeting at the CEA convention in Victoria in 1950, that each of the eight largest provinces (by population) increase its annual grant to the CEA by $150, while the two smallest provinces (by population) pay an increase of $50; if this were agreed to, the CEA might on appropriate occasions, send representatives to conferences abroad. The proposal was approved.[1] Beginning in 1952, therefore, the CEA has been regularly represented at the UNESCO–IBE annual conference. The Association was first represented in 1950, when its secretary, being in Geneva at a meeting preceding the conference at UNESCO expense, remained for the conference.

While the CEA has prepared numerous reports on education for use within Canada and has provided for semi-official conferences and surveys of one kind or another, it is in its relationship to the federal government and to international organizations that the CEA's role has been the most difficult. This has been particularly evident in Canada's relations with UNESCO.

The United Nations Educational, Scientific, and Cultural Organization was established in 1946 as an official inter-governmental agency to which Canada became an early signatory. Even while the formation of this organization was under consideration, CEA records clearly indicate that Association officials were keenly interested in the idea and insistent that the CEA should play a substantial role in Canadian participation.

On November 23, 1945, the secretary addressed the Prime Minister, Mr. W. L. Mackenzie King, drawing to his attention

---

[1]Manitoba does not yet pay a grant for this purpose, and Quebec has paid the grant only recently.

with respect to the proposed establishment of UNESCO a resolution passed by the CNEA directors on November 20, 1945. The resolution stated "that the Canada and Newfoundland Education Association is the only organization representing the departments of education of the provincial governments, which are the legally constituted authorities over education in Canada, and that, as such, the Canada and Newfoundland Education Association is the proper body to be consulted on any educational matter affecting Canada as a whole." Presumably as a result of these and other representations, Dr. G. F. McNally was selected by the Canadian government as one of the five delegates to the UNESCO General Session in Paris in 1946.

In the period since then, the CEA has played an increasingly important role in matters pertaining to UNESCO, though this role has been very much complicated by a number of factors. Among such factors was UNESCO's own unsteady development in a variety of directions, not all of them practical or fruitful, and this aroused the distrust of the Canadian government as well as other governments. However, most countries (sixty-five out of seventy-four by 1955) have established national commissions to advise governments of member states on UNESCO's program and to promote an interest within the states in UNESCO's activities. Canada has not, as is well known, established such a commission. Between 1946 and 1950, many voluntary associations urged the government to recognize the need for a commission in Canada similar to those in other countries. When the Royal Commission on National Development in the Arts, Letters, and Sciences (the Massey Commission) was appointed in 1950, one of its terms of reference was to recommend on methods of conducting Canada's relations with UNESCO. The Commission proposed in 1951 that a Canada Council be established which would, as one of its functions, advise the government on these matters. Although this recommendation has not yet been acted upon, frequent rumors that it will be have served to reduce or divert agitation over Canada's lack of a national commission.

A partial reason for the evasion of action, as stated above, has been the early uneasiness of the Canadian government about

UNESCO as an international organization, succeeded by only a vague interest in it and the formal observance of contractual obligations. Canadian governments have tended to stress the practical and the immediate, rather than cultural affairs. Furthermore, education is a provincial responsibility and, without attempting to explore methods of co-operation by which a commission might be obtained,[1] it has been a convenient refuge for the federal government to say that education is outside its jurisdiction. Canadian voluntary associations have repeatedly pointed out that the same situation exists in the United States, Switzerland, and Australia, but this fact has not prevented the establishment of commissions in those countries.

Yet Canada is a member state of UNESCO, involving correspondence, reports, and government delegations to UNESCO biennial conferences. The procedure that has evolved is that the External Affairs Department, which is the responsible federal government department, consults the CEA on matters pertaining to public education. Provincial departments of education are in agreement with this procedure, and on a number of occasions they have indicated to the CEA that they expect it to serve in this capacity for them. Mindful of the unofficial nature of the CEA, the Association secretary, in dealing with External Affairs, points out that the CEA can serve as a convenient agency if the Canadian government wishes to use it, instead of dealing directly on matters, many of them of a routine nature, with ten provincial departments; at the same time, he has agreed to suggest to the government that it should deal directly with provincial departments of education should a matter arise which would involve important policy or probable controversy. The External Affairs Department seems to find this a helpful arrangement, and as much as a quarter of the secretary's time is taken up with enquiries and reports arising from UNESCO, from other agencies, and from different countries.

While most of the provinces have regarded these responsibilities as properly within the purpose of the CEA, the attitude of Quebec was not so certain; indeed, that province may be said only to have

[1]The Massey Commission recommended that there should be a Canada Council, but not how it should be organized. Federal legislation to establish a Council was passed in the spring of 1957.

acquiesced in this arrangement. However, at the CEA executive meeting on March 25, 1955, the Quebec representative said that he felt that the activities which the CEA office undertook in co-operating with the External Affairs Department were among the things that the province of Quebec expected the CEA to do.

On a number of occasions, the CEA has been dissatisfied with the methods by which Canada's relations with UNESCO are conducted, particularly when the CEA is not kept informed or consulted on certain matters. Since the provinces expect the CEA to keep itself fairly closely in touch with developments in UNESCO, the CEA's dissatisfaction has been drawn to the attention of the External Affairs Department. Among the reasons for the unsatisfactory situation have been the Canadian government's casual interest in UNESCO as an organization, as stated above, the tremendous post-war expansion of Canada's diplomatic service, necessitating very frequent changes of staff on the "UNESCO Desk," and the fact that UNESCO affairs plus all Canada's cultural relations with other countries, including overseas awards and exhibits, are handled by one official with one assistant. These two persons have a multitude of duties, to many of which they can give only cursory attention. Thus, what often appears to the CEA secretariat as indifference to the position of the CEA is often the result, at the operational level, of lack of interest, time, and staff in the External Affairs Department in UNESCO affairs. This explanation does not justify, of course, the Canadian government's relegation of UNESCO affairs to a position where such a situation arises.

Generally speaking, it may be said that the provincial departments of education look upon the CEA as an agency designed to serve their needs and interests, and that the federal government departments, when they have occasion to explore an educational matter with more than one province, frequently find the CEA office a useful point of contact. Thus the CEA is increasingly used as a central office, on behalf of the provincial departments, for various contacts, for the preparation of reports, for replies to enquiries, and for the compilation of opinion. Were it not for the CEA, some other agency, presumably in a federal government department in Ottawa, would of necessity be established for such a task.

Chapter 13

THE ROLE OF THE CANADIAN
EDUCATION ASSOCIATION

In *As You Like It*, the worldly-wise character Jaques says, "And one man in his time plays many parts." The CEA, as has already been outlined, has played a number of parts, though the stage setting was sometimes inappropriate and the cast, until the late thirties, not often a strong supporting one. None the less, circumstances have combined to place certain responsibilities upon the Association, and these in turn do much to determine its principal role.

In the Quance Lectureship (1949), Dr. J. G. Althouse stated: "The first inescapable fact of profound significance (in examining Canadian education) is that education in Canada is a provincial responsibility." Over the years there has been repeated recognition of this "inescapable fact" in innumerable addresses at CEA conventions. On the other hand, while recognizing the autonomy of the provinces, Mr. Vincent Massey, chairman of the Massey Commission and now Governor-General of Canada, once said: "But there must be some means by which these provinces can exchange their ideas—some clearing house of information for this purpose, and also an agency through which to tell the outside world what is going on in Canadian education and to borrow appropriate ideas from outside."

One is reminded of Dr. J. M. Harper's complaint in 1901 that Canada was the only civilized nation in the world unable to tell in co-ordinated fashion the story of its annual educational movements.[1] Some forty-five years later, Dr. C. E. Phillips, having announced his resignation as CEA executive secretary and thereby claiming

[1]See page 65.

freedom from bias, reported to the CEA directors, "My experience with the Association during the past few years has given me the opportunity to judge what the Association has an opportunity of doing. In my opinion there is unquestionably a pressing need for some body to perform functions similar to those of the Office of Education and the National Education Association in the United States. If the executive of the CEA combines tact and caution with vision and energy, and if the provincial education authorities continue to show a generous spirit of co-operation, the Canadian Education Association can play this role of leadership."

Recurrent efforts within the CEA prior to 1918 to bring about the establishment of a federal bureau of education, and the vigorous attempt of the National Council of Education to achieve the same end in the twenties, have served to reveal how unlikely is the creation of such a federal bureau in the near future. When, in 1942, the CEA was faced with an insistent demand from all the national organizations having specific educational interests, that some kind of central educational office, federal or otherwise, be established, the CEA directors decided that the solution lay in setting up their own secretariat in Ottawa. That this secretariat was established instead in Toronto only further reveals the feeling of uneasiness evoked in some areas by the thought of a central education office located in Ottawa.

The Proceedings of the CEA prior to 1942, both the conception and the activities of the Association since then, and the practical measures taken in other federal countries, provide compelling evidence of the need for a central agency in education.

Detailed examples of these activities may be found in presidential addresses to the CEA convention. But the Association is more than a convenient instrument for the provincial departments of education. Increasingly since 1946, local school authorities have attended CEA meetings, have served on the Board of Directors,[1] and have participated in the cost of the central office through membership in the CEA Information Service.

The involvement of urban school officials in the activities and policies of the CEA has had a stimulating influence on the Associa-

[1]Usually the directors of education of five of the major cities are CEA directors.

tion, because it is in the local schools and not in government departments, that the day-to-day work of education takes place. Local school authorities bring to CEA discussions and reports a realism and a sense of immediacy which might otherwise be lacking. As an instance of this, UNESCO recently requested, through the Department of External Affairs and the CEA, the nomination of a Canadian secondary school to participate in a planned experiment in education for international understanding. When the request was discussed at a CEA directors' meeting, a deputy minister volunteered that his province could probably arrange to locate such a school; an urban director of education in the same province thereupon offered one of his schools as a location for the experiment.

Increasingly involved in CEA conventions, and in enquiries directed to the Association office during the year, are large numbers of school trustees. The trustees exchange ideas at CEA meetings, read CEA publications, and, while gaining a broader knowledge of their responsibilities, learn of educational trends and problems in other parts of the country. Simultaneously, the CEA office becomes much better informed on local educational activities and needs.

Representatives of teachers' professional organizations also attend CEA meetings and make considerable use of Association publications. Through the CEA, officials of these influential organizations become personally acquainted with administrative officials from various parts of Canada, to the mutual advantage of both groups.

Representatives of teachers, trustees, the national home and school organization, teacher-training personnel, urban school officials, and departmental officials, all serve on the CEA Board of Directors. In this role, both through the directorate and in annual general conventions, the CEA acts as a national forum to which problems are brought for discussion and clarification. For the role to be effective, it is not necessary that solutions to problems be found, since educational problems in Canada cannot be solved nationally, but only that points of view be brought forward and reconciled, in so far as is possible, in an atmosphere of good faith and mutual understanding.

To round out the complement of educational forces meeting through the CEA, practically all textbook publishers attend CEA conventions and maintain contacts with the CEA office throughout the year.

It will be recalled that the CEA began as a popular assembly of teachers who would meet every two or three years for the discussion of educational problems common to all provinces. This type of organization did not prove to be successful, and the Association was reorganized in 1918 into a small conference of administrative officials in education.

The CEA has since then again evolved into a large popular assembly, truly national, but composed this time of executives and of official representatives of special interest groups in education.

Thus, the history of the Canadian Education Association, and therefore in a real sense the history of interprovincial aspirations in education, suggests four recurring and pressing needs in Canadian education. These are: (1) a central source of educational statistics and of quantitative and measurable material generally; (2) a national forum or meeting place which has some continuity, from year to year, of structure and theme, and at which all attendants have a sense of belonging and involvement; (3) a central agency, under the control of the provincial education authorities, for the somewhat informal collection and dissemination of non-statistical information; (4) a central agency, under the control of the provincial education authorities, for the preparation of formal reports and for joint action or expression of opinion by the provincial authorities on such occasions as circumstances make it desirable or necessary.

The first of these was met, with CEA encouragement and subsequent approval, through the formation of the Education Division of the Dominion Bureau of Statistics. On one or two occasions when the Education Division has exceeded its specific responsibility, there have been criticisms of this expansion of its field. The remaining three needs the CEA has gradually, in so far as its staff and resources would permit, attempted to meet.

The convention, publications, and special committees of the CEA have provided a national forum for the exchange of ideas.

The natural interest of each provincial department of education in educational developments in the other provinces, combined with participation of urban boards in the CEA Information Service, has created a need for the CEA to provide information; considerable progress has been made in making generally available reports on various phases of education, both at the provincial and local level. This role of the CEA, as a central information agency, has been made considerably more effective through its initiation and support of several studies and through the development of the CEA-Kellogg Project in Educational Leadership.

It is in response to the fourth need, that is, in its role as a semi-official interprovincial office of education, that the CEA plays its most important, and at the same time its most difficult role.[1] Every Canadian knows that education is the most sensitive area of provincial autonomy, though all provinces are not equally sensitive. It is probably true now, as it undoubtedly was in the early days of the CEA, that some of the provincial departments of education would welcome the establishment of a federal office of education similar to the offices in the United States and Australia. It is also probably true that the establishment of such an office would be bitterly opposed in some other quarters. For instance, in the much less sensitive area of university, as compared with elementary and secondary, education, the province of Quebec has refused to permit universities in that province to accept the federal grants which were provided on the recommendation of the Massey Commission. Lest this be taken as a purely arbitrary attitude, it should be pointed out that Quebec insists that, since education is by Canada's constitution a provincial responsibility, the federal government should not be in a taxing position where it can give away money for education, while the provinces themselves lack money for this purpose.

Since there is no federal office of education in Canada, there has to be, in this day and age, some sort of Canadian substitute, regardless of how poor, inadequate, haphazard, *ad hoc,* and unofficial such an agency may be. The practices of other countries and

---

[1]For a comparison of the function of a voluntary association with that of an elected legislative authority, see *Canadian Education,* September, 1954, article by F. K. Stewart, pages 54-62.

the relations of these countries with each other require it, and Canada, having the second highest standard of living and being one of the most advanced countries educationally in the world, cannot, simply by ignoring these facts, cause them to change.

Because of this situation and as a result of the events described in this history of the CEA, the Association has come to be an ingenious compromise between the federal office or national offices existing in other countries and no office of any sort, between what some people regard as eminently desirable and others regard as barely possible. Thus the government of Canada is not represented at the inter-governmental conference on public education each summer at Geneva, Switzerland, but the CEA prepares the necessary reports and sends a representative who, as Dr. W. H. Swift has said, is "fully accepted at the Conference and assures that Canada is not among those absent when the roll is called."

It will be noted that Canada is not said to be present but rather that Canada is not absent. This style of construction illustrates rather well the oblique work of the CEA. It is difficult to see how, under the circumstances, it could be different.

Chapter 14

THE FUTURE OF THE CANADIAN
EDUCATION ASSOCIATION

In view of present day speed in travel and communications and its resultant effect upon the movements of persons and ideas, consideration should be given to what lies ahead. Since the establishment of the CEA office in 1945, all the provincial departments of education have accorded the organization warm and ready support. From a permanent staff of two at that time, the number, by 1956, had grown to seven, apart from temporary staff for special projects financed by outside support. With reference to outside support, it should be stated that the CEA, for the ten-year period from 1946 to 1955 inclusive, received from its regular sources of financial support $303,790.51 and from outside sources for special projects $448,936.00.[1]

Through continued support from the W. K. Kellogg Foundation, the CEA's permanent staff, since January, 1957, has consisted of nine persons; encouraging assurance has been given by the provincial departments of education that they will increase their grants in 1961 when Foundation support ends. The small size of the staff indicates that the CEA can perform only modest functions by way of information and liaison. The question therefore arises as to whether so small an agency can meet, as it has been attempting to do, the needs not only of the provincial departments of education but also of Canada as a whole. The writer has some doubt that it can, although on this point, Dr. W. H. Swift has put forward the view: "In all of these respects it seems to me that our organiza-

---

[1]Of this large amount, $266,000.00, as stated elsewhere, was from the W. K. Kellogg Foundation. None the less, the remaining figure is still very substantial.

tion renders a very real service to Canada, and indeed to the provinces, a service which, in these days of rapid travel and varied intercommunication and an enhanced status of our country among the family of nations, must either be carried on through subsidization from the provinces, or, failing that, by some federal agency. Your executive, having regard to the actual cost of such services on behalf of Canada, considered the possibility of asking for some compensation from the federal treasury. In the end, however, it was decided that although many of these things are done for education in a sort of national sense, education is provincial and it is for or on behalf of the provinces collectively that these obligations are assumed, and that if they strain our resources we must look to the provinces to make their assumption possible."

The departments of education are favorably disposed towards the CEA, but their interests are, by their very nature, primarily provincial. One is forced to speculate therefore on how strongly they will continue to insist upon internal autonomy in education and its accompaniment of a needed central agency over which they have control, or whether they will gradually accept a central federal office over which they will have no measure of control but which will be financed by the lush federal treasury. One is reluctant to invoke the popular turn-of-the-century picture of the bird in the gilded cage in a serious essay, but the simile is a fascinating one. At least Quebec and one or two other provinces would not readily agree to such caging.

However, the decision will not be the clear-cut one put forward in the two choices given above; if the question of a federal bureau of education arose today, as it did so often in the CEA in the past, it would probably be rejected. There will be no major decision required in the near future, however, because the question will not arise in that form. What will take place instead will be the making of a number of very small decisions, which, like those of Mr. T. S. Eliot's "tedious argument of insidious intent," will lead in Canadian education to the overwhelming question of whether a federal office should be established. But the answer to the overwhelming question will already have been determined through the acceptance of the various small decisions previously made.

In the writer's view, the probable development will be along the following lines. Education is becoming such a big and complicated business, and the federal government is becoming such a big and all-pervading agency, that it is probable that the latter will become increasingly involved in education. The central government will undertake certain activities of an educational nature because they need to be undertaken, because there will be a vacuum into which the wealthy central government will move either almost unnoticed and unquestioned or perhaps welcomed. The central government will need an agency to co-ordinate and report upon its own activities in education, and such a federal agency will, almost imperceptibly and without any specific decisions being required from the provinces, become the central bureau for all educational activities. Even at present, some reports prepared in Ottawa on education give such prominence to the education of Indians, Eskimos, and inmates of penitentiaries (all federal responsibilities) that foreigners may well wonder if Canadians fall into any other class. Under these circumstances, the role of the CEA might continue to be that of promoting general conventions and of acting as a consultant or advisory committee to the federal office. The tendency of the Canadian government, however, is to set up and control its own advisory committees and to avoid the use of an intermediary agency. Such committees in the Department of National Health and Welfare and other federal departments have followed this pattern.

A second possible development would be dependent upon how deep-rooted is provincial insistence upon their autonomy in education and how strongly they believe in its value, as an educational device, in as wide-spread and varied a country as Canada. It is doubtful that there could be a federal office and hence direct federal aid to public education in Canada without federal control of its expenditure. Arguments that there has not been such central control in ministry grants in the United Kingdom are quite irrelevant, having regard to the difference in British and Canadian traditions in supervising the spending of public funds.

If the provinces resist or are able to keep control of the perhaps inevitable expansion of the federal government into educational matters, and at the same time continue to develop a habit of co-operating in the promotion of matters of common interest and responsibility, they may succeed in developing a unique kind of education office of their own. Remarkable progress has been made in this direction in the past ten years. It may well be that Canada's bi-lingual and bi-cultural nature, and the keen and understandable concern of at least one province towards the preservation of its language, religion, and ethnic origin, provide a situation where an informal, unofficial, voluntary office like the CEA offers the best solution to an extremely complicated problem. Under these circumstances, the several roles of the CEA and the variety in the form of its support offer certain advantages. Since the CEA office depends for its support upon the provinces, it is not possible for it to take action or to express opinion on the relatively few occasions when this is necessary, without first obtaining the consent of all the provinces.

While this situation might seem to make the CEA a weak or frustrated organization, actually it is the source of its greatest strength. Constitutionally, action in Canadian education can take place only by or through the provinces. Constant awareness of this fact strengthens, rather than weakens the central agency, since it is forced to seek the most effective operating procedures within this framework.

The position of Quebec is a special one, which, while accepted, is perhaps not always appreciated. Dr. de la Bruère asked how his colleagues would feel if there were a French-Canadian commissioner of education.[1] In 1943, Dr. Victor Doré, Quebec Superintendent of Education, said that it would be only fair, "when questions of national interest are involved, that all English-speaking provinces should reverse this picture and weigh carefully what their reactions might be were there eight French-speaking provinces and one English . . . Whenever the English-speaking provinces agree to general policies and through courtesy ask Quebec to join them, we naturally wonder what our assent will lead us to, and whether it will or not be binding to further concessions or engagements."

[1]See page 66.

In its work, the CEA tries to take account of the four constant needs in Canadian education mentioned on page 134, and of the practices in educational liaison and information in other countries, of the special problems and attitudes of the French-speaking minority and of other parts of the country as well. It must be sensitive to the fact that some of the provinces are reported to be at the limit of their tax resources for education and that several other provinces are each like a rich Texas. Thus, although Canada's constitution makes each province sovereign in education and Dr. Doré can rightly say,

> Daughter am I in my mother's house;
> But mistress in my own,

it is also true that some of the girls are having trouble with the mortgage payments.

In this complex situation, the CEA tries to recognize that education, though a provincial responsibility, is nevertheless a national concern; the CEA has therefore established a means of communication between the provinces. In the field of reporting information, according to Dr. W. H. Swift, the CEA "fulfils an important and useful function, and in so doing it speaks about Canadian education, not for it." Dr. H. P. Moffatt described the role of the CEA as an interprovincial education office in this manner:

> We can do it in the field of joint action, if we re-member that we represent semi-officially all departments of education and the two major cultures of Canada, and can take positive action only by unanimous consent. This means that we all act together in matters of mutual con-cern; that the majority must forbear from action when the minority considers its fundamental rights are jeopard-ized; that the minority should co-operate, or at least acquiesce, in action on matters that may be of no special interest to it and where no basic principle is at stake.

The way of the Canadian Education Association has not been easy nor the tasks simple. The CEA has reached its present position as an agency of the provinces because Canada's senior educationists have managed to agree upon a procedure of co-operating that goes further than any other procedure conceivable at present in meeting the complex Canadian situation. The CEA office falls far short, in terms of its staff, immediate resources, and official status, of the federal bureau envisaged for many years by some CEA members. On the other hand, it is very doubtful if the federal bureau, controlled by a central government, could have achieved the high degree of unanimity and good will in Canadian education made possible by the CEA, controlled as it is by the provincial authorities who are themselves responsible for education.

Chapter 15

THREE FORMER OFFICERS ASSESS
THE CEA

It seems appropriate, in concluding an account of the development and role of the Canadian Education Association, to have the opinions of several authorities who have been closely identified with the work of the Association. These are the late Dr. J. G. Althouse, honorary secretary-treasurer of the CEA, 1938–43, and often referred to by his colleagues, until his death in 1956, as the "Dean of the CEA;" Dr. C. E. Phillips, secretary-treasurer of the CEA, 1943–45 (part-time), 1945–47 (full-time); and the late Dr. B. O. Filteau, Deputy Minister of Education, Quebec, 1937–55. From 1925 to 1955 Dr. Filteau attended almost every convention of the Association.

The statement by Dr. Althouse and the first statement by Dr. Phillips were obtained expressly for this study of the role of the CEA, and indicate the increasing importance of this Association and its permanent office to Canadian education. The second statement by Dr. Phillips (an address) and the address by Dr. Filteau are slightly abridged versions of addresses they gave at the CEA convention in Quebec in 1955. The former describes, as seen from behind the scenes, the establishment of the CEA office—an operation requiring adroit manoeuvring that will be understandable to careful readers of this book. The latter is a valedictory from a veteran educational statesman who continually supported the work and aims of the CEA within his own province, but who, at the same time, sought and obtained within the CEA a better understanding and appreciation of the problems and philosophy of the province of Quebec.

MILESTONES IN THE GROWTH OF THE CEA

> Dr. J. G. Althouse *was secretary-treasurer of the CNEA from 1938 to 1943; secretary of the CNEA Survey Committee; president, CEA, 1948–49; vice-chairman, Canadian Research Committee on Practical Education, 1949–51; chairman, CEA-Kellogg Project Management Committee and Executive, 1954–56; and Chief Director of Education for Ontario.*

In what follows, I go back only to 1938, because it was in that year I became Honorary Secretary of the (then) CNEA. Before that time I attended some conventions but knew nothing of the real functioning of the Association.

From 1938 onwards, the epochal events (as I see them in retrospect) were:

1. The unprecedented three years' tenure of the president's office by G. F. McNally; the accident of war which produced this long term had very few redeeming features. But this was one. Dr. McNally's aggressive and enterprising temperament made these years, even without a convention, a time of increasing activity in the CNEA office. When a convention could be called, all were agreed that biennial gatherings, as formerly held, would no longer suffice, and the CNEA was launched, willy-nilly, on a policy of constructive continuous service.

2. The challenge of Principal Cyril James (McGill University) was based on an unwarranted assumption that something would be done immediately if only the needs of Canadian education were revealed. The Survey Report was produced by the CNEA, with several momentous results:

    (a) The Association spoke for Canadian education with surprising authority and unanimity.

    (b) In producing the Report, leading Canadian educators worked together with notable patience and enthusiasm.

    (c) In the process, they gained new understanding of one another's problems, and fresh respect for one another's positions. The role played here by B. O. Filteau was significant. Canadian educators not only spoke with one voice;

they established the probability that they could speak with one voice again. This had not previously been suspected. The detail involved in producing such a Report gave ample proof of the need of a full-time secretary and a permanent office for the Association.

3. The genius of Fletcher Peacock for establishing good public relations, and the industry and literary skill of C. E. Phillips, made a unique combination to capitalize on the war-stimulated activity of the Association. The securing of funds for the School Health Survey and the Study of Practical Education made the CEA known far beyond the offices of the provincial departments of education, even to trades unions and chambers of commerce.

4. The permanent secretariat, first under C. E. Phillips, later under F. K. Stewart, developed a vigorous and continuous service for educators. *Canadian Education* and the *Newsletter* supplied general and specific information. The secretary's office became a recognized clearing-house for data to the Canadian government, UNESCO, the International Bureau of Education, the Colombo Plan, and foreign governments. The Association itself undertook specific studies (for example, in the training of teachers) and encouraged co-operation with the Canadian Teachers' Federation, the Canadian School Trustees' Association, L'Association canadienne des Educateurs de Langue française, National Conference of Canadian Universities, and other nation-wide organizations. Research grants-in-aid were made on the recommendation of Canadian universities. The conventions devoted less time to formal addresses and more to discussions and work-shop sessions. Special attention was given to the understanding of French-language education in Canada.

5. The role of the CEA in its relation to the Canadian Government was enlarged, although not fully clarified. The CEA appeared twice before the Massey Commission, and has had active working relations with several departments of the Government of Canada, the Post Office, the Department of External Affairs, the Department of Immigration and Citizenship, the Department of National Health and Welfare, and the Department of National Defence. The Association has never claimed

the exclusive right to speak for Canadian Education; it has pretty well established the principle that the case for Canadian Education is not adequately expressed without some word from the CEA.

6. In the CEA-Kellogg Project, a new pattern has been set. Here the CEA has directly undertaken, with funds secured by the CEA itself, to improve educational leadership. The closer integration of this special project with the work of the CEA office is significant. It probably puts a heavier burden than ever before on the Secretary's staff for the continuous dissemination of information and even implies an obligation for assessment and recommendation, as well. The ability of F. K. Stewart and G. E. Flower to work together, within different frames of reference but with the same general objectives, has been a potent factor in this latest stage of the development of CEA responsibility.

Not the least significant of the consequences of the CEA-Kellogg Project is the extension to the field supervisors of education in Canada of the opportunity for nation-wide consultation and understanding.

THE ROLE OF THE CEA
[A letter to the author]

> Dr. C. E. Phillips *was secretary-treasurer and executive secretary of the CEA part-time from 1943 to 1945 and full-time from 1945 to 1947; chairman, National Committee for School Health Research, 1949–50; has been chairman of the Canada-United States Committee on Education since 1949, and a Director of the CEA; and is a Professor of Education and Supervisor of Graduate Studies, Ontario College of Education.*

My thinking about the role of the CEA begins by answering two questions.

Q. Should Canada have a national office of education supported by the federal government, as in the United States or Australia?

A. Such an office is needed, but its formation does not seem to be practical in our country. The failure of past efforts to establish a federal office is sufficient evidence of the difficulty.

Q. What type of organization might be acceptable to all provincial authorities and might be able to perform most of the functions expected of a federal office?

A. A voluntary organization supported by the provincial education authorities—that is, the CEA.

Obviously, such an organization has no authority of its own. It can speak or act officially on any matter of importance in public education only with the unanimous consent of ten provincial authorities. This limitation makes the CEA appear ordinarily to be an ineffectual body. But on occasion it proves to be the foundation of the rather remarkable prestige the Association enjoys.

The position of the CEA is always precarious, since it must serve ten masters without giving offence to any one. This is a guarantee that the CEA will always be a healthy organization; it is unlikely to outlive its usefulness.

One would have thought that the chief function of the CEA would be research and dissemination of information. Maybe it is. But circumstances and opportunity have led it to engage during the past decade in large scale projects, which somewhat overshadow the routine work of the CEA itself. The time has come, I should think, for the CEA to have its own research department to serve its members in ways that they decide.

I have been asked for comments regarding the choice of Toronto as the location of the office of the Association. At the time the office was first opened, the president (and the executive secretary, to the extent that he was permitted to think aloud) were in favor of Ottawa. But that was because these two promoters hoped to obtain the active co-operation of other national organizations in setting up an education building in the Canadian capital. We were stopped short, not for a lack of promised funds, but by a request for caution from the education authority of one large province. When forced to avert our eyes from Ottawa, we could easily see that Toronto had unique advantages—educationally, socially, and in every other way.

THE CEA ESTABLISHES AN OFFICE

[An address by Dr. C. E. Phillips to the CEA Convention in 1955]

My assignment is to review, in fifteen minutes, events in a four-year period, 1943–47, related to the establishment of the office of the Canadian Education Association. There will be no time even to mention the admirable achievements of stalwarts of the Association before and after.

In 1943, the then Canada and Newfoundland Education Association gained attention and prestige through the publication of its Report of the Survey Committee on the educational needs of Canada. At that time, initial steps had already been taken towards the setting up of a secretariat for the Association. President W. P. Percival had written to provincial ministers of education and received some promises of necessary increase in financial support. But when the directors met before the convention in Quebec in September, 1943, only partial success had been attained in getting the provinces to agree to augment their contributions.

At that convention, nevertheless, a part-time secretary-treasurer was elected. He had the appalling responsibility of succeeding Dr. J. G. Althouse, whose outstanding ability had set a precedent of illustrious service. But if the former incumbent had more of everything else, his successor had one necessary asset—more time. For that reason Dr. Althouse resigned and I was asked to try to fill his place. Fortunately for me, my first president, Dr. V. K. Greer, was above everything else a kindly gentleman who was unfailingly sympathetic and encouraging.

At the same convention, the Constitution of the Association was amended to provide for an executive committee to act for the directors in the interval between conventions, which had become annual only two years before. The president was empowered also to set up a special committee on finance to secure funds for the Association to operate immediately under the new arrangements and to demonstrate that the further expense of a separate office and full-time staff would be justifiable. Under the Honorable Hubert Staines, Minister of Education in Saskatchewan, as convener, the special committee obtained assurance from the provincial governments of annual contributions totalling $7850. This provided a budget in 1943–44 of $2400 for office and travelling expenses, $2000 for research, and $3450 for other expenditures on publications, special committee work, and other activities. The secretarial headquarters of the Association from 1943 to 1945 were in the office of *The School* magazine of which I was managing editor. The CNEA budget enabled me to engage an extra steno- grapher and to delegate certain editorial responsibilities, so that I could devote almost half my time to the business of the Association.

During Dr. Greer's presidency, the work of the Association accelerated smoothly. A committee for the Study of Canadian History Textbooks, under M. l'Abbé Arthur Maheux as convener, met twice and worked steadily. A lengthy mimeographed report was prepared on administrative reorganization in rural areas. The execu- tive committee, as an Educational Policies Committee, prepared for publication *Trends in Education, 1944*. Dr. M. A. Cameron made a study of property taxation and school finance. Numerous special committees worked co-operatively on a variety of matters with other voluntary associations and with government agencies. There was ample justification in October, 1944, for plans to expand the budget to $10,100 in 1945 and to $15,000 in 1946.

Then, on October 13, 1944, Dr. Peacock was elected president and the affairs of the Association were driven forward for two years by the force of Hurricane Fletcher. I say this with no disrespect, but with admiration, affection, and a little awe. Nothing daunted Fletcher Peacock. If the Association had no money, he enlarged his vision to encompass others who had. If his associates on the board of directors demurred at taking vigorous action, he felt it his demo- cratic duty in the name of progress to disregard them. Least of all was he restricted by any jealous or petty consideration for his own reputation or advantage. He was an all-Canadian activist.

To attempt to list in calm chronological order the more im- portant undertakings and advances of the next two years would be to misrepresent the dynamics of a president who was always driving several projects ahead concurrently and who was always on the alert for another venture. One of his favorite enterprises was the Program for the Promotion of Canadian Unity through the schools, which initiated interprovincial pupil correspondence and teacher exchange. A very large amount of time and effort was devoted to an attempt to get war surplus materials for schools; in spite of the major disappointment at the last moment and the very limited incidental success, this was to me the most intriguing campaign of the many we waged. But the president was interested above all in research—not academically, but enthusiastically. After meetings of the directors and at other opportunities—sometimes at one o'clock in the morning—he would come into my hotel room and lecture to me for an hour on the importance of research for education and the need for far-sighted vision.

During the first of his two years of office, the president met on the train a representative of the Canadian Life Insurance Officers Association. He discerned a means of bringing to realization plans for research which had been no more than a topic for discussion in previous years. Months of negotiation intervened—but only months. In June, 1945, Dr. Peacock was able to announce that the life insurance companies of Canada were prepared to contribute through the Canadian Life Insurance Officers Association $10,000 for the first year of a proposed five-year program of research to be conducted by the National Committee for School Health Research. The Committee was to be sponsored jointly by the CNEA and the Canadian Public Health Association but to be under the administrative supervision of the CNEA. At the same meeting of the executive committee, President Peacock also announced that the CNEA from September 1 would have an office of its own and a full-time secretary-treasurer and staff.

The concurrence of the two announcements was not mere coincidence, although one was not the preceding cause of the other. The progress of the Association to its new status was accomplished pragmatically by interaction of forces. Ventures led to achievements which brought money which made possible other ventures which ensured support for the first venture. This process scared me at first. It looked as if any slowdown might land us in jail. But actually there was no risk because Fletcher Peacock never allowed anything to slow down for long—not even the secretary. In the minutes of the executive committee dated April, 1945, it is written that consideration was given to modifications in plans made necessary by the smaller amount of money available that year and the reduced prospects for 1946. But two months later the Association was soaring ahead on a new wing and a new air of optimism.

Some people think it takes money to open an office, but they suffer from what Fletcher Peacock called lack of vision. We looked at space for rent in a few buildings, but decided in favor of a large room on the top floor of Ryerson Public School graciously made available gratis by the Toronto Board of Education. A few plywood screens divided our space into semi-detached suites for the CNEA and the National Committee for School Health Research, of which Dr. A. J. Phillips was director. Alec and I found that the office arrangements had the advantage of making any electric intercommunication system unnecessary. We acquired a typewriter, filing cabinets, tables, stenographers' desks and chairs, and other office equipment by the process known as scrounging—the victim or benefactor being in this case a provincial government which would probably prefer to remain nameless. By a monetary interaction process which I would shudder to explain even now, we were able to buy an additional typewriter, two desks, and two chairs. We paid for our telephone. We engaged two stenographers. We were in business.

During his second year of office, President Peacock launched new ventures and sighted new sources of revenue. Reports actually published in 1944–45 and waiting publication by the fall of 1945, made it plausibly economical to begin publication of a quarterly in October, 1945, and *Canadian Education* appeared. The president began the lengthy series of conferences which were to culminate in a second major research program; and he began actively to plan for enlisting the support of local school boards. Let me reassure you that in spite of the imagination used in raising money, we were actually extremely careful about spending it. At the end of President Peacock's second year of office, in August, 1946, we had a net bank balance of close to $5000, although even the budgeted contributions from the provinces had risen by that date only to a total of roughly $10,000 a year.

In August, 1946, Dr. B. O. Filteau became president of the Association under its new name, the Canadian Education Association, and under its new constitution which provided more suitably for our increasing co-operation with other educational bodies. No better choice of a president could have been made at this stage of the Association's growth. We had plenty of momentum; we needed only a gentle hand at the reins to direct our course. We had made many sit up and take notice; we needed the confidence of all and the esteem which comes when caution and urbanity direct an active enterprise. Dr. Filteau provided these qualities. Under him, we continued to progress with little diminution of speed, and with dignity.

There is time to mention only four events of the year 1946–47. (1) The Association had made tangible contributions to the work of UNESCO, and in the fall of 1946 was invited by the federal government to nominate a representative to the UNESCO general assembly—Dr. G. F. McNally. (2) During the winter, the president, the past president, and the executive secretary succeeded in getting twenty school boards to contribute about $3000 a year to the Information Service, which was formally inaugurated in the spring, although it had been operated for some months to provide an argument for getting the money to bring it into existence. (3) In May, also, the president was able to announce that the Canadian Research Committee on Practical Education was ready to begin work, with a budget of $15,000 a year based on commitments secured from a number of different organizations. (4) The contributions from the provinces were increased to $15,000 a year.

Another good stroke of business was our employment of Mr. F. K. Stewart to succeed me as executive secretary at the end of my leave-of-absence from the Ontario College of Education. Freeman and I worked together in the office during June, 1947; and the affairs of the Association were safe in his capable hands when I left in July to fill engagements at the University of Maine and with UNESCO in Paris.

The title of President Filteau's address to the convention at the end of his year of office in September, 1947, was *An Abundant Harvest*. Graciously and with extreme modesty, he gave most of the credit to others for the achievements of the Association and for its sound position. He outlined the many activities through which the CEA had gained financial support, which would total no less than $50,000 for the year that lay ahead.

Dr. Filteau would probably fail to do justice to his own work on behalf of the Association, but let me remind you that he was a keenly interested and active director and officer during the years of which I have been speaking and that he was the one chiefly responsible for the consolidation of resources—the achievement most needed in the year of his presidency, 1946–47.

A QUEBEC VIEWPOINT

> Dr. B. O. Filteau *was Deputy Minister of Education for the Province of Quebec from 1937 until 1955; vice-president of the Canadian Association for Adult Education; a member of the Canada-United States Committee on Education; and president of the Canadian Education Association, 1946–47.*

It will be thirty years ago next November that I had the honor to be delegated for the first time, as a representative of my province, to a meeting of this Association which was then known as the Dominion Education Association.

I had been appointed only two weeks before as Assistant to the French Secretary of the Department of Education for this province and I possessed only superficial notions concerning our rather complicated school system. When I was called upon to report for my province regarding educational developments during the preceding year as it was customary to do at that time, I stood up with great apprehension and thought it wise to seek salvation in a humble confession of my ignorance and inability.

My good friend, Mr. Stewart, our executive secretary, had the kindness to send me some time ago an excerpt of my modest remarks which he had extracted from the proceedings of the 1925 convention and, with your kind permission, I will just quote a few lines of what was, so to speak, my maiden speech before this Association.

> "Ladies and Gentlemen, before attempting to summarize the development of education during the past

scholastic year, I feel it my duty to transmit to you the message of hearty greetings and cordial good wishes with which I have been entrusted by the Superintendent of Education for the province of Quebec. The Honorable Mr. Delâge also requested me to express to you his deepest regret that he could not attend this meeting. With Dr. Parmelee away to preside at this convention and our French Secretary also absent on a business trip, it was impossible for Mr. Delâge to confide the care of the whole department to the new Assistant Secretary, who has been in office only a few days and who has the honor of addressing you at the present time. But, having little use at the home office for the new member of his staff, Mr. Delâge thought it wise to let him have the privilege of attending this conference and thus give him an opportunity to make a most fruitful use of his time. I should be in extreme embarrassment if I were the only representative of my province, but fortunately Dr. Parmelee and Mr. Sutherland are here and will be at hand to correct or supplement the few notes which I have hurriedly prepared."

I then went on with my little report which I now realize was quite unequal to requirements.

As an encouragement for my effort, perhaps, but more probably because I was the only representative of French Canada, I was appointed the next day as a member of the Board of Directors, an honor of which I have been ever since, the unworthy beneficiary.

Since that first meeting in 1925, I have attended almost every one of the conventions of this Association and, as years have passed by, I have made not only charming acquaintances but reliable and faithful friends in every part of Canada.

My chief objective during these thirty years has always been the same: "Education and good understanding," or better, "Good understanding through education."

For many years, I felt somewhat dubious as to the result of my humble work towards this objective. For almost twenty years, I stood alone as representative of French Quebec and in spite of the unfailing sympathy and courtesy of my English-speaking colleagues from all over Canada, I could not defend myself from a feeling of uneasiness and loneliness.

But in 1944, when the question of a permanent secretariat arose, I felt very happy to have by my side, in Toronto, Mgr Aimé Labrie, Vice-Rector of Laval University, and several delegates of the Montreal School Board headed by Mr. Trefflé Boulanger, Director of Studies.

That meeting of 1944, in Toronto, should be counted as one of the most important in the history of this organization. Then and there was found a definite and satisfactory solution to the critical and often-times discussed question of the establishment of a federal bureau of education.

Instead of a federal bureau, whose very name had raised energetic opposition in several instances, from some provinces, it was unanimously agreed, after long discussion, to establish an interprovincial bureau under the direction of a full-time executive secretary.

At the same time, in order to clarify the status and the aims of the Association, a statement was issued under the title: *The Canadian Education Association—What it is—What it does,* stressing the fact that the Canadian Education Association is an interprovincial body comprising first of all representatives of the various departments of education and endeavoring, with due respect to the constitutional rights of each province, to promote education throughout Canada.

After ten years of experience, I am pleased to say that the establishment of this permanent secretariat has done more than anything else for the development of co-operation and good understanding across Canada. Whereas, until 1945 the various provinces had been subscribing yearly only a few dollars, as it were, for the maintenance of the Association, they were, from 1945, called upon to make a per capita contribution which amounted to several hundred and even in the case of the larger provinces to several thousand dollars. The fact that all provinces have accepted the new plan of support and that, since then, their yearly contributions have been more than doubled is unequivocal evidence of the interest taken and importance attached by them to the work of this secretariat. . . .

Through its various functions and services, in the fields of research, information, teacher exchange, external relationships, and particularly through the workshops organized under the CEA-Kellogg project for the benefit of our school inspectors or superintendents, this permanent secretariat has greatly facilitated the interchange of correspondence and personal contacts and has brought together from every province a considerable number of educators and administrators who otherwise might never have had an opportunity to exchange their views and become responsible partners in a national enterprise.

This partnership in the great task of education cannot fail to develop in our minds and hearts a feeling of mutual trust and friendship, together with a spirit of reciprocal aid and respect which we in turn shall endeavor to instil as fundamentals into the minds and hearts of all young Canadians. May I say, on bidding farewell to you, that it is with deep contentment that I look forward to this result which has been my constant aim as a member of this Association.

Constitution of the Canadian Education Association, 1946

ARTICLE I—NAME
The Association shall be called the Canadian Education Association.

ARTICLE II—AIMS OF THE ASSOCIATION
1. To bring about a better understanding on the part of each province and of Newfoundland of the educational ideals of each, to the end that with due regard to constitutional rights the cause of education may be promoted in all.
2. To collect and make available to educators in Canada and Newfoundland information on educational developments in Canada and elsewhere.
3. To foster educational research in Canada and Newfoundland and to publish reports of selected research studies.
4. To collaborate with other educational organizations, and to function as a co-ordinating agency.

ARTICLE III—MEMBERSHIP
1. Individual membership in the Canadian Education Association shall be open:
   (a) to any professional educator employed in any educational institution or school system controlled or recognized by any provincial department of education, or by the Department of Education in Newfoundland;
   (b) to any person interested in education who is a member of any group or association mentioned in Section 3 below, or who is a member of any organization affiliated with any group or association mentioned in Section 3 below;
   (c) subject to the approval of the directors, to any other person engaged in education or in work connected with education in Canada or Newfoundland;

(*d*) to all life members and honorary presidents of the Canadian
Education Association.

2. Individual members shall have the right to attend all sessions of
the Association and to join in the discussion. They shall also be
entitled to receive the regular publications of the Association and
to request educational information from the Secretary-Treasurer.

3. Representative delegates to the annual convention of the Association shall be individual members designated as representatives by
educational agencies, groups and associations in Canada and Newfoundland, as follows:

(*a*) a maximum of seven representatives from each of the departments of education in the nine provinces of Canada and in
Newfoundland;

(*b*) a maximum of four chief executive officers or superintendents
employed by school boards in each province and in Newfoundland, such representatives to be chosen by the chief executive
officers or superintendents of their respective provinces who
are present at the meeting of the Association;

(*c*) a maximum of four representatives of teacher-training institutions in each province and in Newfoundland, such representatives to be chosen by the teacher trainers of their respective provinces who are present at the meeting of the
Association;

(*d*) one representative each of the following institutions engaged
in educational research:

(i) The Department of Educational Research, Ontario
College of Education,

(ii) The Education Branch of the Dominion Bureau of
Statistics,

(iii) L'Institut pédagogique St.-Georges,

(iv) Any other research institution approved by the Board of
Directors;

(*e*) a maximum of four representatives of the supervisory or inspectoral staffs of each province and of Newfoundland, the
representatives to be chosen by the provincial association of
supervisory or inspectoral personnel where such an association
exists; where no such association exists the representatives to
be chosen by the supervisors or inspectors of their own
respective provinces who are present at the meeting of the
Association;

(*f*) two representatives each of the Canadian Teachers' Federation
and of the Newfoundland Teachers' Association; and two
representatives of each provincial federation of teachers;

(g) one representative of the Canadian Trustees' Association and of the Newfoundland Trustees' Association; and one representative of each provincial association of school trustees;

(h) one representative of the Canadian Federation of Home and School and one representative of each Provincial Federation of Home and School;

(i) one representative of the Canadian Association for Adult Education and one representative each of such provincial associations for adult education as may be approved by the Board of Directors up to a maximum of two representatives from each province;

(j) one representative of the National Conference of Canadian Universities, and one representative each of all Universities in Canada and of the Memorial University College of Newfoundland—the representative of any university to be the executive head of the institution or person named by him;

(k) one representative each of other national or provincial educational associations or agencies whose applications for representation are approved by the Board of Directors;

(l) all life members and honorary presidents of the Canadian Education Association.

4.   Representative delegates, as individual members, shall have the rights described in Article III—2. At the time of the annual convention they shall also have the right to vote on resolutions, to elect the officers of the Association as provided in Article IV—1, and to amend the constitution of the Association as provided in Article VIII.

ARTICLE IV—OFFICERS

1.   (a) The officers of the Association shall consist of one Honorary President from each province represented in the Association and one from Newfoundland, the immediate Past President of the Association, a President, a Vice-President, and twenty-four other Directors. Six of these Directors shall be: the president of the National Conference of Canadian Universities or a representative named by him;[1] the president of the Canadian Teachers' Federation or a representative named by him; the president of the Canadian Federation of Home and School or a representative named by him; the president of the Canadian School Trustees' Association or a representative named by him; the president of the Canadian Association for Adult Education or a representative named by him; and the chairman of the

[1]Deleted in 1947.

Canadian Council of Education for Citizenship or a representative named by him. Subject to the provisions of section 1 (b) below, twenty[1] Directors, including the President and Vice-President, shall be elected by ballot, unless otherwise arranged by unanimous consent, on a majority vote of the representative delegates present at a regular meeting of the Association, and shall hold office until the next regular meeting.

(b) No election of Directors shall be valid unless each province and Newfoundland are represented on the Board of Directors.

2. The officers of the Association, with the exception of the Honorary Presidents, shall form a Board of Directors. This Board shall have power to fill all vacancies in its own body arising in the interval between regular meetings; it shall have in charge the general interests of the Association; it shall conduct the business of the Association between the regular meetings of the Association, and shall make all necessary arrangements for such meetings.

3. The Board of Directors shall name from its membership an Executive Committee of five.[2] This Committee shall be composed of the Past President, the President, the Vice-President, and two additional members. This Executive Committee shall act in an advisory capacity to the President and shall take such action as circumstances may require in the interval between meetings of the Board of Directors.

4. It shall be the duty of the President to preside at all meetings of the Association, of the Board of Directors, and of the Executive Committee. In his absence the Vice-President shall preside and in the absence of the Vice-President a *pro tempore* Chairman shall be appointed on nomination, the Secretary-Treasurer putting the question.

5. The Secretary-Treasurer shall be a paid official of the Association. He shall be appointed by the Board of Directors and shall be responsible to it. He shall—

(a) carry out undertakings approved by the Board of Directors and the Executive Committee,

(b) conduct all official correspondence of the Association, the Board of Directors, and the Executive Committee,

(c) keep an accurate account of the proceedings of the meetings of the Association, of the Board of Directors, and of the Executive Committee,

(d) receive and under the direction of the Board of Directors hold in safe-keeping all monies paid to the Association,

[1]Increased to twenty-three in 1949.
[2]Increased to six in 1955.

(e) make payments in accordance with the orders of the Board of Directors,

(f) keep an accurate account of his receipts and expenditures on behalf of the Association,

(g) submit a full statement of receipts and expenditures for audit when directed to do so by the Board of Directors.

Additional duties may be assigned to the Secretary-Treasurer by the Board of Directors. He shall be bonded by the Board of Directors.

ARTICLE V—MEETINGS

1. The regular meetings of this Association shall be held annually at such places and on such dates as may from time to time be determined by the Board of Directors.

2. Special meetings of the Association may be called by the President at the request of not less than ten members of the Board of Directors.

3. Each newly-elected Board of Directors shall hold a meeting following the close of the regular meeting of the Association at which it was elected.

4. Other meetings of the Board of Directors shall be held at the call of the President.

ARTICLE VI—FEES

The annual individual membership fee shall be two dollars, and shall be payable on the first day of January.

ARTICLE VII—APPOINTMENT OF COMMITTEES

By the first day of May of each year, the President shall appoint the following committees:

(a) on Honorary Life Memberships

(b) on Resolutions

(c) for Nominations

(d) for any other purpose deemed expedient by the Board of Directors.

ARTICLE VIII—AMENDMENTS TO CONSTITUTION

This Constitution may be altered or amended at a regular meeting of the Association by a two-thirds vote of the representative delegates present, provided that written notice of motion of the alteration or amendment has been given at least forty-eight hours before the session at which the motion is to be considered.

Article IX—Audit

An annual audit shall be made by a chartered accountant, appointed by the Association at its annual convention. The fiscal year of the Association shall be from January 1st to December 31st next following.

APPENDIX B

Chronological List of Conventions

CONVENTION	PLACE	DATE	PRESIDENT	SECRETARY
1	Montreal	July 5–8, 1892	1891–1892 Hon. G. W. Ross Minister of Education, Ontario	Rev. E. I. Rexford Secretary, Protestant Council, Quebec
2	Toronto (jointly with OEA)	Apr. 16–18, 1895	1892–1895 Hon. G. W. Ross	Rev. E. I. Rexford
3	Halifax	Aug. 2–5, 1898	1895–1898 A. H. MacKay Superintendent of Education Nova Scotia	A. McKay, Halifax
4	Ottawa	Aug. 14–16, 1901	1898–1901 J. A. McCabe Principal, Ottawa Normal School	J. T. Bowerman[1] Ottawa
5	Winnipeg	July 26–29, 1904	1901–1904 D. J. Goggin Superintendent, Northwest Territories, Regina	W. A. McIntyre Winnipeg
6	Toronto	July 10–13, 1907	1904–1907 John Millar[2] Deputy Minister of Education Ontario	D. J. Goggin, Toronto

[1]Resigned through ill-health at end of convention. M. E. Conway was appointed Acting Secretary.
[2]Millar died in the interval, and Vice-President McIntyre became President.

CONVENTION	PLACE	DATE	PRESIDENT	SECRETARY
7	Victoria	July 13–16, 1909	1907–1909 Alexander Robinson Superintendent of Education British Columbia	J. D. Buchanan Normal School Vancouver
8	Ottawa	Aug. 20–23, 1913	1909–1913 J. W. Robertson Principal, Macdonald College	C. J. Lynde Professor of Physics Macdonald College (To Jan. 1912) J. A. Dale Professor of Education McGill University (Jan. 1912–Aug. 1913)
9	Ottawa	Jan. 31–Feb. 2, 1917	1913–1917 J. W. Robertson	J. H. Putnam Inspector of Schools Ottawa
10	Ottawa	Nov. 20–22, 1918	1917–1918 W. S. Carter Superintendent of Education New Brunswick	J. H. Putnam
11	Ottawa	Nov. 1–3, 1922	1918–1922 F. W. Merchant Director of Technical Education Ontario	J. H. Putnam
*				
13	Ottawa	Nov. 10–12, 1925	1922–1925 G. W. Parmelee Director of Protestant Education Province of Quebec	J. H. Putnam

*There was no twelfth convention.

CONVENTION	PLACE	DATE	PRESIDENT	SECRETARY
14	Winnipeg	Nov. 1–3, 1927	R. Fletcher Deputy Minister of Education Manitoba	J. H. Putnam
15	Montreal	Nov. 5–7, 1929	F. H. Sexton Director of Technical Education Halifax	J. H. Putnam
16	Toronto	Nov. 6–8, 1934	J. T. Ross[1] Deputy Minister of Education Alberta	W. J. Karr Director of English Instruction, Ontario Department of Education
17	Regina	Oct. 19–21, 1936	G. F. Rogers Chief Inspector of Secondary Schools, Ontario	W. J. Karr
18	Halifax Saint John Charlottetown	Aug. 15–19, 1938	H. F. Munro Superintendent of Education Nova Scotia	W. J. Karr[2]
19	Ottawa	Aug. 27–29, 1941	G. F. McNally Deputy Minister of Education Alberta	J. G. Althouse
20	Victoria	Sept. 15–17, 1942	S. J. Willis Deputy Minister of Education British Columbia	J. G. Althouse

[1] H. H. Shaw, Vice-President, Ross resigned in the interval, and Shaw presided as President at convention in 1934.
[2] Karr indisposed at this convention. F. L. Woodley made acting Secretary.

CONVENTION	PLACE	DATE	PRESIDENT	SECRETARY
21	Quebec	Sept. 14–16, 1943	1942–1943 W. P. Percival Director of Protestant Education Province of Quebec	J. G. Althouse
22	Toronto	Oct. 11–13, 1944	1943–1944 V. K. Greer Superintendent of Elementary Education, Ontario	C. E. Phillips
23	Edmonton	Aug. 20–22, 1946	1944–1946 F. Peacock Director of Education New Brunswick	C. E. Phillips
24	Quebec	Sept. 11–13, 1947	1946–1947 B. O. Filteau Deputy Minister of Education Province of Quebec	C. E. Phillips F. K. Stewart
25	Winnipeg	Sept. 28–30, 1948	1947–1948 A. R. Lord Principal, Vancouver Normal School	F. K. Stewart
26	Fredericton	Sept. 13–15, 1949	1948–1949 J. G. Althouse Chief Director of Education Ontario	F. K. Stewart
27	Victoria	Oct. 2–4, 1950	1949–1950 L. W. Shaw Deputy Minister of Education Prince Edward Island	F. K. Stewart
28	Saskatoon	Sept. 18–20, 1951	1950–1951 M. E. LaZerte Dean of Education University of Alberta	F. K. Stewart

CONVENTION	PLACE	DATE	PRESIDENT	SECRETARY
29	Toronto	Sept. 16–18, 1952	1951–1952 H. P. Moffatt Deputy Minister of Education Nova Scotia	F. K. Stewart
30	Halifax	Sept. 15–17, 1953	1952–1953 C. C. Goldring Director of Education Toronto Board of Education	F. K. Stewart
31	Edmonton	Sept. 14–16, 1954	1953–1954 G. A. Frecker Deputy Minister of Education Newfoundland	F. K. Stewart
32	Quebec	Sept. 20–23, 1955	1954–1955 W. H. Swift Deputy Minister of Education Alberta	F. K. Stewart
33	Winnipeg	Sept. 26–28, 1956	1955–1956 Allan McCallum Deputy Minister of Education Saskatchewan	F. K. Stewart

Bibliography

For references to the conventions and history of the Canadian Education Association, the main sources of information have been the Proceedings of the Association under its various names:

Dominion Educational Association, *Proceedings*, 1892–1917

Canadian Education Association, *Proceedings*, 1918–1936

Canada and Newfoundland Education Association, *Proceedings*, 1938–1944

Canadian Education Association, *Proceedings*, 1946–1955

Further sources of material for the general development of the CEA have been the minutes of the meetings of the directors and of the executive, and the official journal of the Association, *Canadian Education*, published quarterly since 1945. A study has also been made of the files of the Association, somewhat sparse prior to 1945, but more than adequate since that date.

For information on the National Council of Education, in addition to bulletins, circulars, memoranda, and documents of a miscellaneous nature, the following sources have been consulted:

National Council of Education, *Proceedings*, 1919, 1922, 1929

NCE, *The National Council of Education—Its Constitution and Purpose*, 1922

National Conference on Education and Citizenship, *Education and Life*, 1923

The development of the Research Council has been traced with the assistance of the minutes of the Canadian Council for Educational Research, 1938–1944, and of the CEA Research Council, 1945–1955, and also *Canadian Council for Educational Research*, a report published by the CNEA in 1944.

For the study of educational liaison in other countries the main references have been:

UNESCO, *World Survey of Education*, 1955

UNESCO, *Directory of Education Clearing Houses,* 1955,
        (mimeographed)
United States Office of Education, *Handbook of the Office of
        Education,* 1955
United States Office of Education, *To Promote the Cause of Edu-
        cation* by L. Blauch (reprinted from *School Life*)
Commonwealth Office of Education, Australia, *Annual Report,* 1954
Australian Council of Education Research, *Annual Report,* 1953–54
Other material used in this section has come from correspondence
with the International Bureau of Education, Geneva, and with the
Secretary, Swiss Standing Conference of Heads of Cantonal Depart-
ments of Education.

Other miscellaneous sources of information for this study of the
history and role of the Canadian Education Association have been:
Provincial Association of Protestant Teachers of Quebec, *The Edu-
        cational Record,* 1891–1895 issues
Canada and Newfoundland Education Association, *Report of the
        Survey Committee,* 1943
CEA, *The Status of the Teaching Profession,* December, 1948
The Year Book of Education, 1952 (Chapter on Canada)
J. G. Althouse, *Structure and Aims of Canadian Education*
Publications of the CEA-Kellogg Project

INDEX